AFRICAN CHRISTIANITY
patterns of religious continuity

STUDIES IN ANTHROPOLOGY

Under the Consulting Editorship of E. A. Hammel,
UNIVERSITY OF CALIFORNIA, BERKELEY

AFRICAN CHRISTIANITY
patterns of religious continuity

Edited by

George Bond
Teachers College
Columbia University
New York, New York

Walton Johnson
Livingston College
Rutgers University
New Brunswick, New Jersey

Sheila S. Walker
School of Education
University of California
Berkeley, California

ACADEMIC PRESS
A Subsidiary of Harcourt Brace Jovanovich, Publishers
New York   London   Toronto   Sydney   San Francisco

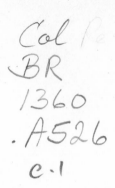
ACADEMIC PRESS, INC.
111 Fifth Avenue, New York, New York 10003

United Kingdom Edition published by
ACADEMIC PRESS, INC. (LONDON) LTD.
24/28 Oval Road, London NW1 7DX

Library of Congress Cataloging in Publication Data

Main entry under title:

African Christianity.

(Studies in anthropology)
Includes bibliographies and index.
1. Christianity——Africa——Addresses, essays,
lectures. 2. Christian sects——Africa——Addresses,
essays, lectures. 3. Africa——Church history——
Addresses, essays, lectures. I. Bond, George C.
II. Johnson, Walton R. III. Walker, Sheila S.
BR1360.A526   289.9   79–51668
ISBN 0–12–113450–4

PRINTED IN THE UNITED STATES OF AMERICA

79 80 81 82   9 8 7 6 5 4 3 2 1

TO ARTHUR H. FAUSET

author of *Black Gods of the Metropolis,*
one of our intellectual predecessors

CONTENTS

LIST OF CONTRIBUTORS

Numbers in parentheses indicate the pages on which the authors' contributions begin.

George C. Bond (137), Department of Philosophy and the Social Sciences, Teachers College, Columbia University, New York, New York 10027

Walton Johnson (89), African Studies, Livingston College, Rutgers University, New Brunswick, New Jersey 08903

Bennetta Jules-Rosette (109), Department of Sociology, University of California, San Diego, La Jolla, California 92093

Leith Mullings (65), Department of Anthropology, Columbia University, New York, New York 10027

Sheila S. Walker (9), School of Education, University of California, Berkeley, Berkeley, California 94720

FOREWORD

By that mysterious influence which is imparted to man independently of outward circumstances, to not a few of them the preaching of the gospel, defective as was its practical implication, opened a new world of truth and goodness.
—EDWARD R. BLYDEN, 1876

It is with a keen sense of pride that I introduce this collection of essays on the subject of African Christianity. Not the least of my reasons for pride in this book is that the contributors represent a generation of young Afro-American scholars with whom I have been associated, whose anthropological training and field research have brought new insights to the interpretation of African religious experiences. Another reason is more personal in nature. As I read these essays the significance of the religious coefficient in Pan-Africanism was brought home to me most forcefully, so much so that I once thought, in a moment of contemplation, that the book might have been entitled "the variety of African religious experiences," to paraphrase William James. And I might have gone on to suggest the subtitle: "the historical antecedents of Pan-Africanism and the role of religion in it." In taking such license, that is, in suggesting an alternative title for this book, it was not my intention to inflict violence on its theme nor to register a sense of uneasiness with it. But it did seem to me that the Lumpa Church of Zambia, the Harrist Church of the Ivory Coast, and the Vapostori Church of Zaire, as well as other African Christian congregations described in these pages, stand as bold testimony to the prophetic visions of such nineteenth-century champions of Pan-Africanism as Bishop Henry McNeal Turner and

Edward R. Blyden.[1] It was with this in mind that I chose to preface
these introductory remarks with a quotation from Blyden's *Christianity, Islam and the Negro Race.* Writing an introduction to that
collection of Blyden's essays and speeches, the historian Christopher
Fyfe described how Blyden had prophesied the "evolution of African
Churches freed from the burden of European precept and example."[2] *African Christianity* conveys the message that prophecy does
not inevitably fail.

Let me hasten to say that these original essays on variant forms
of African Christian belief and worship in West and Central Africa
are not aimed at vindicating the prophecy of Edward R. Blyden, a
black, ordained Presbyterian minister, whose disillusionment with
Christian missionary activity, then operating under the protective
umbrella of colonial domination of Africans, led to visions of an
"Africa for Africans," to use his words. Rather, these five studies of
indigenous African Christian religious initiative "freed from . . . European precept and example," singly and collectively, make contributions of the first order both to the comparative sociology of religion
and to the history of religions.

There is both sociological and hermeneutical value in the term
"African Christianity." At the conceptual level, it establishes a rational framework, setting the evolution of African churches squarely
within the historical pattern of the rise and spread of Christianity as
a world religion. By viewing African Christianity as a historical and
sociological variant in the development of Christianity, the authors
avoid the conceptual bind imposed by conventional terms found in
the anthropological literature on the consequences of the missionary
effort in Africa. "Independent African Church," "African Prophetic
Church," and similar terms seem to be firmly entrenched in the sociological language used to describe Christian forms of African belief
and worship, but typological labels such as these have little intrinsic
merit; they smuggle in the notion of homeostasis when, in fact, religious continuity and change occurs, as these essays plainly demon-

1. Edward R. Blyden, *Christianity, Islam and the Negro Race,* 1887. Edited by
George Shepperson (Edinburgh: Edinburgh University Press, 1967). For the best scholarly
accounts of the religious element in the Pan-Africanism of Bishop Henry McNeal Turner, as
expressed through the missionary activities of the African Methodist Episcopal Church in
southern Africa, see Carol A. Page, "Henry McNeal Turner and the Ethiopian Movement in
South Africa." Unpublished M.A. Thesis, Roosevelt University, Chicago, 1972; "State and
Church Reaction to the A.M.E. Church in Transvaal and Cape Colony, 1896-1910." Unpublished Ph.D. Dissertation, Edinburgh University, 1978.
2. Christopher Fyfe, "Introduction" to *Christianity, Islam and the Negro Race,* p. xiii.

strate. Apart from connoting a latent ethnocentric bias, terms like "African Prophetic Church" tend to be heavily burdened with the freight of "religious deviancy"; they attribute to African churches a kind of religious pathology, a weakening of European "orthodox" Christian precepts. No more satisfactory are the familiar sociological labels "sect" and "cult." Applied to the organization and the theological doctrines of African churches, the terms "sect" and "cult" gloss over developments in Christian religious history that African churches have been very much part of. These religious-historical developments need to be kept in perspective. But all too often sociological observations on the emergence of African Christian churches fail to set this phenomenon against the historical backdrop of modern Christendom.

In the first century of Christendom, religious unity, as manifested by theological and doctrinal consensus, was a spiritual ideal early Christians rarely achieved in practice. Under the leadership of self-proclaimed "prophets" and "saints," "independent churches" were made up of small flocks of religious devotees, who most often expressed their religious beliefs fanatically. This was the normative state of affairs, not the exception. Among the writers who have viewed transformations in early Christendom from an anthropological perspective, Anthony Wallace has pointed out that Christianity was transformed from "a millenarian, apocalyptic Jewish sect led by the fanatical Messiah Jesus, into a Gentile Graeco-Roman sect led by Paul, and eventually into the giant institutions of the Roman church."[3] These early transformations through time and space have continued to the present day, showing both constancy and change in Christian thought and practice. Religious currents generated by experimentation in early Christian thought and practice spread beyond the continent of Europe and influenced the development of Christianity in Asia Minor and Africa. As we now know from the historical record, among the Greek, Latin, Syrian, and Egyptian branches of early Christianity there were diversities arising from the variety of national cultures onto which Christianity was grafted. Theological rifts led to charges of heresy. For instance, among the most important theological disputes in which early Christians engaged was how to define the mystery of the Incarnation. Unable to settle the question at the Council of Chalcedon in 451, the Greco-Latin Church clung to the belief that Christ had within himself two natures, divine and hu-

---

3. Anthony Wallace, *Religion: An Anthropological View* (New York: Random House, 1966), p. 254.

man. The Syrian, Armenian, and Egyptian churches held fast to the Monophysite belief that the two natures were fused into one. Contemporary historians of religion view these theological disputes, to say nothing of controversies over the spiritual role and authority of church leadership, as chapters that led to the variant forms of modern European and Near Eastern Christian belief and worship. A comparative sociological perspective, which takes account of the sociocultural factors underlying these early developments in European Christianity, views them as not very dissimilar in religious form and content from twentieth-century developments in African Christianity.

Although the emergence of the Lumpa Church of Zambia, the Vapostori Church of Zaire, and other African churches represent latter-day developments in the spread of Christianity in Africa, the *African* antecedent of indigenous Christian religious activities was rooted in the founding of the ancient Ethiopian Church. In the whole of black Africa, only the Ethiopian Church, which began as a province of the Egyptian Coptic Church in the fourth century A.D., constitutes a chapter in the history of early Christendom; African Christianity as described in these essays constitutes a chapter in the history of modern Christendom.

I cite the example of the emergence of the Ethiopian Church because I take it to be a precursor of latter-day developments of Christianity in Africa. Born in the fourth century from European Christian missionary efforts that in religious dogma and practice were not unlike those used among unconverted Africans in the twentieth century, Ethiopic Christianity in time evolved into an institution with a distinctive cultural stamp. In its liturgy and liturgical language, its forms of worship and church service, its local saints and martyrs, Ethiopic Christianity today bears little resemblance to its early Egyptian Coptic antecedents; African Christianity, uprooted from its European missionary foundations, has also evolved its own local cultural forms. A myriad of historical, political, and social factors, to say nothing of cultural factors, combined to shape the distinctive style of what we now observe as Ethiopic Christianity. And although Ethiopian Christians belong to one of the oldest Christian churches in the world, European missionaries still arrive in Ethiopia armed with their own religious formulae and stratagems for carrying out the work of the Lord. Their spiritual mission is to convert Ethiopian Christians to Christianity!

African Christianity, like Ethiopic Christianity, is Christianity. Both emerged out of an expanding "world-system" at different periods of historical time. Ethiopic Christianity arose from the impetus of an expanding Greco-Roman world; the European colonial system gave rise to twentieth-century African Christianity. Despite its political and economic priorities and objectives, the European colonial system was not entirely a secular system. White and black Christian missionaries were also part of that system. Between the years 1844 and 1853 white missionaries like Johan Ludwig Krapf made the first serious attempts to introduce modern Christianity to East Africa;[4] a few decades later black American missionaries of the African Methodist Episcopal Church labored in central and Southern Africa,[5] a continuance of black American mission activity in Africa that had begun on a small scale with the establishment of a Baptist church in the new British settlement of Sierra Leone in 1792.[6] In their religious zeal to convert Africans to the new faith, white and black missionaries exploited indigenous African religious belief systems. They furthered the aims of their home missions by offering to the unconverted heavenly rewards in the bye and bye. Acting on behalf of their national governments, colonial administrators exploited indigenous political and economic systems by offering to traditional leaders and public figures terrestrial rewards in the here and now.

In the late twentieth century, African political leaders, not colonial administrators, make use of party politics and other political instruments for acquiring power and authority to shape human and natural resources to meet the demands placed upon the state by a changing secular world. In this same period, European missionaries have lost their standing to African religious leaders like John Maranke, Alice Lenshina, and latter-day followers of John Harris, all of whom occupy a central place in the essays in this collection. Now it is they who make use of the particular forms of religious belief and worship peculiar to their brands of African Christianity as instruments to aid their congregations in adjusting to the demands placed upon them by a changing spiritual world.

Religious systems are social systems, Sir Raymond Firth once

4. An outstanding figure in the Church Missionary Society, London, Krapf undertook serious missionary work in East Africa after having experienced dismal failure in his efforts to convert to Christianity the Galla, in Ethiopia between the years 1837–1844. See J. Lewis Krapf, *Travels, Researches and Missionary Labours During an Eighteen years' Residence in Eastern Africa,* 1860. (London: Frank Cass, 1968, 2nd ed.)

5. See Carol A. Page, "Henry McNeal Turner."

6. This was the work of a former slave, David George, who became "the first American Negro minister in Africa." See George Shepperson, *Independent African: John Chilembwe and the Origins, Settings and Significance of the Nyasaland Native Rising of 1915* (Edinburgh University Press, 1958), p. 99.

said, and a change in one leads to a change in the other. Plainly, the varieties of African Christian religious experience reflect the social, economic, and political changes African societies have undergone, especially since the mid-nineteenth century. The introduction of new economic systems, including wage labor employment; the dislocation of rural folk from the hinterlands and from the relatively secure traditional life, which accompanied the growth of urban and peri-urban centers; the spread of literacy through formal and informal education, setting the stage for the emergence of social classes which reinforce social inequality between the privileged few and the deprived masses — all these weigh heavily upon the ways in which Africans perceive their universe and their place in it. At the level of the belief system, alterations occur in their cosmological system, including pantheon and myth and belief about existence, which correspond to changes in their social system. And it is in this arena of religious thought and change that *African Christianity* makes a further contribution to the sociology of religion. By advancing beyond the ordinary anthropological descriptions of the structural arrangements of African church congregations, the study provides first explorations into the belief, ritual, and symbolic content of African Christian cosmology. Here there is grist for the mills of contemporary anthropological investigations of religious systems, most recently in the writings of Mary Douglas on the concept of "grid and group" and the discussion by Sir Edmund Leach of the dialectic in practical religion. These essays enable us to view the variety of African Christian religious experiences against the background of the social conditions and historical circumstances in which they arose. We now stand on firmer intellectual grounds than heretofore for conceptualizing the broader problem of religion and society in the latter-day Age of Imperialism in Africa.

We shall never know if Edward R. Blyden would have been pleased with how the imperfect preaching of the gospel in the nineteenth century opened a new world for African Christians in the twentieth century. To be sure, the African churches through which the Christian religion is now expressed have in fact been freed from the "burden of European precept and example." With this, doubtless Blyden would agree.

William A. Shack

INTRODUCTION

African Christianity has arisen within the context of an expanding "world-system" (Wallerstein 1974) and, thus, it bears the imprint of this Western system. European colonial expansion set the stage for the rapid spread of Christian missions and for the rise of a multiplicity of African prophetic movements, sects, and churches. At the same time that Africans were being brought into an overriding economic system, they were also being exposed to a world religion that had itself contributed to the rise of capitalism in Europe (Weber 1930; Tawney 1944) and provided an essential ideological component in European colonial expansion.

The European conquerors made use of Christianity in such a manner as to buttress their position of political and economic dominance, to promote their ideas within the new colonial states, and to define a new position for Africans in relation to wealth and power. Under their rule autonomous African polities were integrated into unitary imperial systems. Africans were being transformed into a "common people" (Cole and Postgate 1961) who, while being integrated rapidly into the demands of a world economic system, remained subordinate to the regional centers of European colonial

1

AFRICAN CHRISTIANITY
Patterns of Religious Continuity

governments. The notion of a common people in Africa draws attention to that segment of the population which is at the periphery and is the recipient of centralized authority and power. Specifically it refers to those who are powerless, lacking in special privileges or status and any significant degree of control over land or their own labor. They toil, for example, as laborers, peasant farmers, clerks, and traders. They are for the most part simply the working folk. The notion of an African common people may be said to have two dimensions. The first draws attention to the political and economic position of a contemporary population, and the second to the historical processes which have produced a common laboring force, one which owes its economic and political subordination to European colonial expansion. This second dimension is concerned with the making of an African common people as well as the formation of new social classes. The same complex forces which have contributed to the making of a common people and to new social classes in Africa have also led to the development of African Christianities different from the Christianity of European rulers.

African Christianity became a religion of an emerging common people who shaped it and were in their turn shaped by it. It is noteworthy that the Republic of South Africa should contain such a large number and such a variety of African Christian movements. Barrett indicates that half of the 6000 "independent" churches in Africa are in the Republic (Barrett 1968). South Africa has the largest number of industrializing urban centers, a large wage-earning population, and it is under the firm rule of a small European ruling class which uses Christianity to justify its dominant position. Although both rulers and ruled accept Christianity, this common acceptance has not necessarily produced a coherent, compatible, or complementary religious system. This observation suggests the truism that Christianity is a general rubric for a wide range of religious movements and that only a universal theory of religion would be able to explain the particular cases represented in this volume.

The various forms of African Christianity, both the missionary churches that preserve essentially the same form and content in Africa that they have in Europe, and the newly created Africanized versions of Christianity, provide a series of intellectual bridges, of recognizable ideological statements, which different strata may claim as an encompassing reality. It is quite possible and acceptable for the socially mobile to change their church affiliation without producing social or ideological dislocations, a not unusual pattern among upper and lower class and urban and rural populations in Africa (Porter 1953;

Murphree 1969). Political independence may not affect the pattern of religious distribution. Minor civil servants, teachers, clerks, political leaders, and the university educated intelligentsia have moved smoothly into positions vacated by the European rulers, often preserving their Christian beliefs and practices and enshrining them in political ideologies such as Humanism. Johnson's discussion of the African urban elite in Lusaka, who belonged to the African Methodist Episcopal Church, provides a clear example (Johnson 1977) as does Walker's account of the national recognition accorded to the Harrist movement in the Ivory Coast.

The African Christian Churches are part of a dynamic and continuous historical process of religious innovation involving both the evolution of internal factors and the absorbing of external influences which are molded to fit the current realities of a given social, cultural, or political movement. Few movements may be expected to arise in conjunction with changing social, economic, and political realities, just as the contours of the existing ones have been and will continue to be modified as a result of such factors.

Thus African Christianity is undergoing constant changes as a product of human experiences and as part of the interaction of economy and society (the same observation may be made of Christianity in Europe and America). Monica Wilson emphasizes the importance of this interaction in her theory of social change (Wilson 1954 and 1971) and more specifically in recognizing the necessity of observing how "religion changes as hunters become herders, or cultivators," or as herders and cultivators become machine minders (1974:4). In Maine's terms, contract is rapidly displacing status as the dominant principle of social relationships in many spheres of the African's daily life as peasant and worker. Urbanization, industrialization, and a market economy based upon cash have introduced contractual arrangements into the small rural community. While African religions such as ancestor worship will not necessarily disappear, it would seem that their range may be increasingly constricted or restricted to particularistic relationships based on status. At the same time the principles of contract contained in Christianity, a universal encompassing religion, may be extended, especially as the scale of social relationships changes. Thus, while "traditional" religious beliefs and practices such as ancestor worship and witchcraft may form part of the urban setting, as religious expression they may cluster around or accrete to particularistic relationships which conform to "traditional" patterns anchored more in status than in individual contract.

The five chapters that make up this volume are studies in practical religion (Leach 1968:1) or living Christianity. They do not constitute explorations into philosophical religion. There is thus an expected discrepancy between the theological dimensions and "the religious principles which guide the behavior of an ordinary churchgoer," as Leach has so astutely pointed out. These chapters present the practical attributes of a mundane Christianity and no attempt is made in them or in the Discussion to construct an African theology according to "Western philosophical terms" (see Benjamin Ray's observation on this attempt, 1976:14-16). We do however recognize that the works of African theologians will affect the growth of Christianity in Africa, not solely its philosophical properties as a world religion but also its practical dimensions as a folk religion. It is this latter aspect as a folk religion that provides for its dynamic and transmutable quality. So as one has the making of an African common people, a new peasantry, a new working class, a new elite, so also are new religions in the making, and it is these living, practical religions that this collection of ethnographic cases represents.

II

The chapters that make up this volume trace the development, growth, and spread of five African Christian movements from their initial conceptions to their present situations. Attention is given to changes in the societies in which these movements are found and to the extent to which these changes have influenced the structure, organization, and beliefs of each movement. Each author's analysis presents a different theoretical and methodological perspective—always, however, based on the premise that the point of reference is the African social and religious context. The chapters offer the basis for critical looks at earlier formulations about such institutions in the light of both new data and new analytical frameworks.

Thus one may not expect to find uniformity in conceptual and theoretical formulations. We suggest that this order of intellectual diversity provides one of the rich features of the volume as well as generating internal controversy among the chapters. The contributions range widely in theory, some employing a poststructural analysis while others derive their theory from a Weberian action frame of reference; religion in its cultural and ideational perspective takes precedence over the materialist foundation of social relationships and religious belief. This view in its turn is challenged from a more materialist orientation, one which questions idealist assumptions as the basis of providing satisfactory explanations of religious behavior.

In the first chapter Sheila Walker traces the rise of the Harrist movement from its genesis in Liberia to the present status of having one of its branches recognized as one of the national churches of the Ivory Coast. The Harrist Churches in themselves are a microcosm of diversity. They illustrate the subtle complex principles found in many African Christian movements. These churches represent the results of a prophetic movement which proliferated into a variety of dissimilar churches and sects because of the form and content of the Prophet's message and the ways in which it was disseminated, interpreted, and implemented.

The Harrist movement has a number of distinctive features. The Prophet William Wade Harris preached Christianity and prepared his followers to join Protestant and Catholic mission churches. Walker systematically traces the various prophets and cults which sprang from the movement based upon the interpretation converts gave to Prophet Harris' behavioral and verbal message. She also describes the manner in which the Harrist movement adjusted to local custom and practice. The Harrist Churches themselves constitute a wide spectrum of Christian movements which are African rather than European-mission insprired.

The Church of the Messiah is one of the many "spiritualist churches" that have sprung up in twentieth-century Ghana, with a major emphasis on healing and seeking protection from misfortune. Leith Mullings explores themes of religion and social change with respect to Christian movements in Labadi, a small Ga town in Ghana. She argues that the Church of the Messiah reflects the development of social class ideologies in the town, and in so doing has helped to undermine relationships based upon descent and furthered those based upon class. The values manifest in the church doctrine and activities are in line with the development of relationships based on social contract required by the need to deal with the world beyond one's lineage, one's town, and one's ethnic group.

The African Methodist Episcopal (A.M.E.) Church did not originate on African soil and has the unique characteristic of being a Black American mission church. Walton Johnson analyzes the adaptive and functional character of the African Methodist Episcopal Church in Zambia. He demonstrates that although it is technically a mission church, the A.M.E. Church functions as an African institution. Johnson examines the A.M.E. Church as a voluntary association that provided a new urban elite with new principles, values, norms, relationships, and social skills. He argues that the A.M.E. Church prepared its members to deal with the new social order of a plural society that was experiencing rapid urbanization. Both its initial success and its later decline are explainable, to a large degree, in terms of its functioning in the context of social change.

The Apostolic Church of John Maranke, or the Vapostori Church movement is, like the Harrist Churches, a prophetic movement in which the prophet is dead. It is a church that has a centralized structure which attempts to maintain control and authority while directing growth. Bennetta Jules-Rosette traces the rise of Maranke's Vapostori Church from its humble beginnings in rural Southern Rhodesia to its emergence as a multiethnic, international African Church. She considers the problems arising from growth and explores the relation of the church center to its outlying congregations. She examines a dispute between two Zairean church leaders for control over local congregations. At the headquarters the Rhodesian leaders settle disputes by prophetic judgments based upon visions. This mode of arbitration allows for the continuation of local schisms within the context of the Church and, thus, for the Church's expansion. Both the Vapostori and the Harrist movements are examples of successful and growing African Christian movements.

It would be inappropriate to contrast prophetic movements such as the Harrist and Vapostori and the Church of the Messiah and Lumpa on the basis of whether the founding spiritual leader is dead or alive. The fact that the spiritual founder of a prophetic movement is alive is, of course, temporary. But while he is still alive these Christian movements do tend to retain a personal, particularistic organizational character that prevents them from developing into formal organizations in which universalistic attributes predominate. Crucial for the spiritual and organizational coherence of a movement are the procedures allowing for the succession of the prophet, the spiritual focus of the movement. Scale alone produces tensions between parochial, particularistic tendencies and universalistic ones, and between adherence to spiritual values and the pragmatic demands of maintaining an effective organization. These types of tensions may be mediated through the person of the prophet while he is alive. An immediate crisis affecting the integrity of the movement is produced by the death of the founding spiritual leader; while it may lead to schism, as is the case of the Vapostori Church, it may also produce religious growth and expansion.

George Bond describes the Lumpa Church of Zambia as a case of a prophet who failed. The Lumpa Church is also a prophetic church whose founder constituted the direct spiritual and organizational authority. Bond traces the rise of Alice Lenshina Mulenga, the founder of the Lumpa Church, and explores the relationship of that Church to the government and the dominant political party. In explaining the structure, organization, and beliefs of a local Lumpa congregation, Bond argues that the Lumpa Church was basically a fundamentalist, reformist Christian movement whose members attempted to withdraw from the secular world.

These chapters provide an indication of the diversity of African Christian movements while elucidating the fact that they exhibit many common features. The movements provide responses to similar kinds of situations, often arriving, however, at different solutions as a result of the particular circumstances of their origins and evolution.

The goal of the volume is to provide broadly comparative data, emphasizing common themes and concerns and the ways in which these relate to each other. In the Discussion that follows the chapters, the editors suggest new approaches to the study of African Christian movements based on the ethnographic presentations. There are several major themes that have important analytical, theoretical, and methodological implications.

Of central importance to the understanding of these religious movements is the manner in which they take root, gain adherents, and spread. These cases demonstrate the significance of Africans as those who spread the gospel or created new religious movements. A most vivid example of this process is the role of the prophet who was at the center of several of these movements in their initial phases. But African Christianity had much to encompass, and thus another central theme is the manner in which these African Christian movements deal with "traditional" beliefs and practices, providing, we may suggest, new justifications or bases for making, as well as restricting, choices among the alternatives created in a situation of rapid social change. These movements were not only part of the process of change but also were often themselves catalysts to change, and thus we explore the new beliefs and practices which they propounded to their adherents.

The contributions comprising this volume describe the movements at different phases in their development raising the question of the reasons for their different patterns of progresssion. Although they have their own internal dynamics as religious organizations, these movements also have secular functions as voluntary associations within the community. Hence they are directly related to the phenomena of class formation, ethnicity, and the rise of various forms of nationalism. The setting of the unfolding of African Christianity may also have a geographical component. Each chapter explores these movements within their rural, semiurban and urban environments as well as their relation to their economic and political circumstances.

REFERENCES

Barrett, D.B. 1968 *Schism and Renewal in Africa.* Nairobi.
Cole, G.D.H. and Postgate, R. 1961. *The British Common People.* New York: Barnes and Noble.
Johnson, W. 1977 *Worship and Freedom: A Black American Church in Zambia.* London: International African Institute.
Leach, E. (ed.). 1968 *Dialectic in Practical Religion.* Cambridge.
Murphree, M.W. 1969 *Christianity and the Shona.* London: The Athlone Press.
Porter, Arthur T. 1953 "Religious Affiliation in Freetown, Sierra Leone." *Africa,* Vol. XXIII.
Ray, B.C. 1976 *African Religions.* Prentice Hall.
Tawney, R.H. 1944 edition *Religion and the Rise of Capitalism* (first published 1926).
Wallerstein, I. 1974 *The Modern World-System.* New York: Academic Press.
Weber, M. 1962 *The Protestant Ethic and the Spirit of Capitalism.* London: Allen and Unwin Ltd. (first published 1930).
Wilson, M. 1971 *Religion and the Transformation of Society.* Cambridge: Cambridge University Press .

I
Sheila S. Walker

THE MESSAGE
AS THE MEDIUM
The Harrist Churches
of the Ivory Coast and Ghana

THE PROPHET AND HIS MESSAGE

In 1910, the native Liberian William Wade Harris had a vision in his prison cell of the Angel Gabriel. Gabriel's message to Harris was that he had been designated as God's last prophet whose mission was to carry His Word to those people who had not yet heard it. Those people who did not heed the message would soon be destroyed by fire. This event was at the origin of a mass movement that revolutionized the religious life of most of the southern Ivory Coast.

William Wade Harris was born in Graway, Liberia, about 1865, near the Ivory Coast border, of non-Christianized, traditionally oriented Grebo parents. He was sent to live with and be instructed by a fellow Grebo who was a Methodist minister and director of a school. There Harris learned to read and write both Grebo and English and was baptized a Methodist. After a few years Harris, like many other young Grebo men, went to work as a member of the crew of one of the British ships that plied the West African coast and had the opportunity to visit other African countries. Upon his return he married and became a lay minister in the Methodist Church.

The Methodist missionaries in Liberia catered particularly to the

9

AFRICAN CHRISTIANITY
Patterns of Religious Continuity

Afro-American settlers although there were native Liberians, like Harris's host, who occupied important positions in the church. Missionaries from the Episcopal Church, also present in Liberia, directed their activities specifically to the native Africans. Shortly after their arrival the Episcopalian missionaries devised a system of writing Grebo and began to translate hymns, prayers, and parts of the scriptures into that language. Episcopalian church services were held in Grebo, native ministers were trained and ordained, and schools were set up to make people literate both in their own language and in English.

While Harris was a young man the Grebo became disaffected with the Liberian government because of what they considered treaty violations, a situation that led to four wars between the Grebo and the government in the latter part of the 1800s. Having had experience with British shipping companies, and many of them having visited British colonies as crew members, some Grebo leaders wished to be administered by the British rather than by the Liberian government.

Harris became a partisan of this position. His leaving the Methodist Church for the Episcopal Church was perhaps reflective of this change. In the Episcopal Church also he became a lay minister and later became a teacher and then director of a boarding school. He also worked for some time as an interpreter for the Liberian government, in which capacity he was expected to act as a peacemaker between antagonistic factions among the Grebo. Instead he led one Grebo faction against another that he felt to be too favorably disposed toward the government. For this he lost his government position.

One day in 1910 Harris led a group of Grebo in an act symbolic of their attitude toward the Liberian government. In a public square he removed the Liberian flag and replaced it with the British Union Jack. For this act he was suspected of being part of an alleged coup d'état plot and was imprisoned for treason. While in prison he read his Bible and prayed a good deal. In this context the vision occurred that changed both his life and the religious life of the southern Ivory Coast.

Upon his release from prison Harris began to preach what he said he had been told by the Angel Gabriel, but in Liberia he met with ridicule. He had an outfit made for himself consisting of a long white gown with black bands crossed across the chest and a little round white hat, perhaps inspired by pictures of biblical prophets.

Carrying with him a gourd rattle, a gourd bowl for baptismal water, a tall staff in the form of a cross, and his Bible, Harris and two similarly attired female companions set off to the east, toward the French Ivory Coast colony, to pursue the new Prophet's mission.

When Harris arrived in the Ivory Coast at the end of 1913 the French were finishing their program of "pacification." The area had been made a colony in 1895 as a result of treaties signed between the French and the chiefs of the coastal ethnic groups. The initial policy of the colonial administration had been "peaceful penetration," in which the French tried to win the loyalty of their new subjects by presenting themselves as protectors without shows of military force. Starting in 1908 the policy was changed when the newly appointed governor observed that very little of the territory was actually under French control. Military tactics were then put to use until 1915 when the colony was judged pacified. Some ethnic groups required more force than others to be subdued. The coastal ethnic groups and those around the lagoons near the coast, such as the Ebrié, Alladian, Avikam, and Adjoukrou, who had experienced some positive benefits from the European presence, were less resistant than the inland forest groups like the Dida, Abbey, and Attié, who put up a fierce struggle.

The imposition of colonial status was disruptive of the indigenous societies. A money economy was established, which created new bases for wealth and prestige, and people were forced to work in industrial plantations and public works projects and to pay a head tax. Roads were built and people were regrouped from small settlements to large villages along the new roads. Missionaries were summoned to provide education for the colonial subjects in order to make them loyal to France and more useful to the colonial establishment. The missionaries attacked elements of the indigenous social organization and religious system. They wanted the Africans to give up the religious sytem that the Europeans considered "devil worship" and they considered the polygamous family to be sinful. The missionaries did get some villages to cease the overt practice of their traditional religion with the promise to teach them Christianity, which the Africans imagined to be a stronger religion because it had given the Europeans the power to conquer them. However, after having given up their traditional form of worship, some of the villages came upon hard times and, finding that the Christian practices taught by the missionaries did not preserve them from misfortune, returned to their old practices. The missionaries in the Ivory Coast had the assistance of the colonial officials in their attack on the indigenous religions because in many cases it was the traditional priests who led their people in opposition to the French.

The Prophet Harris succeeded, where the missionaries had not, in persuading people to give up their indigenous form of worship. Whereas the Catholic missionaries who had been in the colony for the past two decades had succeeded in baptizing only a few hundred people, Harris baptized what colonial administrators estimated at 100,000 to 120,000 people in about 1 year, the overwhelming majority of whom took the baptism as the beginning of their lives as Christians and either joined the missionary churches or sought to practice Christianity on their own.

Most of the Prophet's time was spent among the lagoons' ethnic groups between Grand Lahou and Bingerville, although he made a brief foray of several weeks into the southwest of what was then the British Gold Coast colony (now Ghana), where he also met with phenomenal success. In the Ivory Coast he was kept under close surveillance and was imprisoned on at least one occasion by colonial officials suspicious of a foreign African who drew great crowds of their subjects, many of whom came from distant areas to hear him. Some colonial officials assumed that Harris's intent was to create political unrest detrimental to the administration. He was summoned for audiences with both the governor of the colony and the superior of the Catholic mission, both of whom were unaware of his antigovernment political activities in Liberia. The governor, after talking with Harris, concluded that his intentions were not political, which all evidence suggests was correct, and determined that his activities were acceptable. The Catholic superior, although he disagreed with Harris's methods, appreciated him because the number of people seeking to join the mission churches had been increasing by leaps and bounds since the Prophet had begun directing his converts to them. In the Gold Coast Harris had led people to the Protestant Churches, whose rolls also increased phenomenally as a result of his influence.

Harris's technique was that he and his followers would enter a village singing songs and accompanying themselves with gourd rattles. When a crowd gathered Harris would preach his message. If people agreed to renounce their former religion and worship as Harris preached, he would baptize them with water from his gourd bowl, placing the Bible on their heads. The acceptance of the baptism was understood as a commitment to the new god. Sometimes priests or priestesses of traditional gods would become possessed by these deities when they came before Harris. The Prophet would invite them to touch his cross and would sprinkle them with his holy water, which would chase away the deity and calm the person.

The essence of Harris's message was that people should abandon their traditional religions and worship the Christian god exclusively. They must destroy all religious objects and cease all behavior relating to the traditional deities, whose worship constituted a sin before the new god for which a convert would be promptly and thoroughly punished. It is said that when Harris entered some villages, the buildings in which the traditional religious objects were kept burst into flames, and that in others the gods who were worshipped told their priests that they had to leave because a stronger god was coming along. People who accepted Harris's baptism while trying to retain some objects associated with the traditional gods for security are said to have been immediately struck dead by the Christian god.

The essence of the meaning of Harris's activities lay largely in his baptism. The leader of the Catholic mission told Harris that he had no authority to baptize and that baptism should succeed, not precede, religious instruction, as was the Catholic practice. Harris responded that the mission with which he had been charged by his god was to baptize people in preparation for religious instruction. The baptism was to purify them of the sins they had committed in the past and to act as a preservative to protect them from harm, particularly during the period of transition from the old religion to the new, while they were learning to be proper Christians. Harris understood that the Africans could not be expected to give up their traditional religious protection for the mere promise of a stronger protection that was to come only after a period of instruction during which they would have no protection at all. In the traditional religious system water had been used for purifying baths and to prevent and cure illness and misfortunes. It was within this framework that the Prophet's baptism was understood by his converts.

In a number of villages Harris was not readily accepted at first, and traditional priests pitted the strength of the gods they represented against Harris, which gave the Prophet the opportunity to prove the superior power of his god by thwarting the local priests. Harris's prestige grew as he was believed to have worked a number of miracles. The door of the cell in which he was imprisoned was said to have opened of its own accord, and a colonial official who mistreated the Prophet and died shortly thereafter was believed to be the victim of Harris's god's wrath for his act. In addition, he was said to have healed with his holy water people judged incurable by traditional healers, and one village that would not heed his message was said to have been attacked by baboons and another to have found itself in total darkness although the sun shone brightly all around. After such demonstrations of Harris's power whole villages allowed themselves to be baptized, usually led by their religious and political leaders. The traditional religious leaders often became the leaders of the new religion. Thus the new religion fitted into the traditional structure with little organizational disruption.

In addition to worshipping one god, Harris converts were exhorted to respect the Sabbath absolutely, and there are dire stories about people who did not take this precept seriously. His message also included some more secular teachings such as the prohibition of theft, lying, adultery, and drunkenness. He tolerated polygamy but said that monogamy was preferable.

Harris was not the first person who had come to the lagoons area preaching about a new god who was more effective than the old gods in assuring health and prosperity and protecting people from evil. Others had preceded him who taught local people to serve gods whose influence sometimes spread over large areas as they gave proof of their effectiveness. Harris was understood as fitting into the pattern established by these predecessors, and his ritual accoutrements were perceived in the same way as the traditional religious objects and acts that they resembled. Although he would break his cane cross in public and remake one of local materials to indicate that the object contained no power in itself, the cane cross was still believed to contain a strong spirit. The gourd rattle was believed to imprison evil spirits inside, and the baptismal water was thought to have curative powers once it was blessed by Harris. The Prophet told people that the truth of his god was contained in the book he carried. Parents should therefore send their children to school to learn to read so that they could read the Bible to their elders in order that the latter might know God's will.

Harris told his converts that in order to learn to be good Christians after his baptism, they should go to the churches available and should build their own houses of prayer where there were none. These latter should be led by a minister and 12 apostles designated by the village community. In many cases far away villages sent delegates to hear the Prophet, be baptized by him, and return to share the new religious teachings with their fellow villagers. This was one of the ways in which Harris's teachings penetrated to areas that he did not visit.

Another way in which Harris's message was spread and his teachings perpetuated was through the activities of Methodist clerks from

Sierra Leone and the Gold Coast who were working for British trading houses in the Ivory Coast. Harris designated some of these men as his disciples and they went to places Harris never reached to carry his message and baptize people. They also provided rudimentary teachings for some of the people whom Harris had baptized and taught them the Ten Commandments, the Lord's Prayer, and Protestant hymns. Some visited converted villages and led or assisted with church services on a more or less regular basis.

The Prophet Harris also told his converts that "teachers with Bibles" would come to teach them the contents of the book and how to be good Christians. Since he referred some of the people he baptized to his designated disciples, they may well have been the "teachers with Bibles" to whom he was referring. In 1924, a Protestant missionary came to the Ivory Coast because the French were not allowing the English-speaking Protestant Africans living in the colony to worship freely. To his great surprise and pleasure he encountered tens of thousands of people who claimed to be "Harrist Protestants" waiting for "teachers with Bibles." He hurriedly gathered together a number of Protestant missionaries to respond to their request for guidance, providing more of the "teachers with Bibles" whom Harris had said would come.

THE MOVEMENT AFTER HARRIS

By the end of 1914 the French colonial administrators had decided that although the Prophet's current intentions might be purely spiritual, should he decide to take any political stand he could easily mobilize their African subjects against them. They were particularly sensitive about this possibility since they were just beginning to feel that their own control over the colony was well established. Also, it was the beginning of World War I, and both French colonial personnel and African subjects were being mobilized for the war effort. This factor both weakened the power of the administration and further alienated some of the ethnic groups that, in addition to having lost their sovereignty, were also losing their men. For these reasons, the Prophet Harris was repatriated to Liberia. He tried to return to the Ivory Coast on several occasions to continue his work, but was prohibited from doing so by border guards.

Before Harris's expulsion the Methodist clerks he had appointed as his disciples had become very active in continuing the Prophet's activities. He had given cane crosses like his own to some as symbols that they were to continue his mission, and some he had empowered indirectly. A Methodist trader from the Gold Coast who was living in the village of Audoin sent the Prophet a message requesting that he come to the village to baptize people. Unable to accommodate him, Harris sent the man a Bible and requested that he share his Christian knowledge with the other villagers. A Catholic, Victor Nivri, from the Alladian village of Addah, requested and received permission to baptize from a man named Brown who had been made a disciple by the Prophet. People from different ethnic groups began to come from afar to be baptized by Nivri. An assistant of Brown's known only as Papa was also very active in the Grand Lahou area, and probably baptized several thousand of the converts attributed to Harris (Haliburton 1971: 70, 94–95). Other disciples carried Harris's message into the interior to areas that the Prophet never reached. It appeared that people were as receptive to the disciples as to the Prophet Harris himself because they had heard that there was a great man preaching about a new god and were anxious to learn to worship him. It seems probable that most people, having no more precise knowledge, thought that the disciples were Harris himself, particularly since many of them wore white outfits like Harris's, carried a cane cross and English Bible, baptized in the same way, and were also English-speaking.

The administration had distinct reservations about the proliferation of these disciples, particularly since most were from British colonies and had no allegiance to France at a time when the French colonial government was trying to inculcate a sense of loyalty to the metropole among its subjects. In addition, as Harris's message was spread inland by the disciples and by the delegates from distant villages who had come to see him, and as rumors spread about the great man and what he could and would do, the content of his message was understood differently by different groups. The religious content was distorted in some villages. An administrative report of the time noted that in one village in which the people claimed to be practicing the religion of the Prophet Harris, a shrine had been built upon which sat a bottle of water believed to have magical powers. The water was used to chase witches. In other areas the Prophet's message was understood to have more political content. Some groups believed that Harris would rid them of the French. One rumor said that a lion from Libera would come to devour the Europeans.

A memo dated December 16, 1914, from the Lieutenant-

Governor of the Ivory Coast colony to all administrators, said of this situation:

> From information coming to me from different sources, it appears that the moral-improving activity of the "prophet" William Wade Harris is interpreted in a different fashion by the natives and is hampered in a rather unfortunate way mainly by his imitators, improvised pastors recruited from among clerks severed, often for delicate reasons, from their counters.
>
> So it is that one administrator has told me about the rumor circulating in his *cercle* [administrative district] that Harris was going to succeed in obtaining before long a reduction in the rate of tax and even the suppression of the *capitation* [head tax].
>
> In the impossible situation in which the much reduced personnel from the *cercles* now find themselves, the doings of these more or less religious personages (we do not really know who they are or where they come from, or what are their real intentions) cannot be watched closely enough, therefore you will invite the pretended "sons of God" who have been roaming to the villages recently to return to their own country where they will be able to spread the good word easily. The Prophet Harris in particular will find in Liberia, his own country, a sufficiently vast field for activity [Quoted in Haliburton 1971: 139].

After Harris's repatriation his disciples tried to continue to spread his message, and other "prophets" inspired by Harris's successful example came on the scene. Some easily gathered followers among the multitude of people whom Harris had convinced to abandon their traditional religion and who, having learned only the rudiments of the new one, were seeking new religious leadership in a style suggested by the Prophet. Many, however, were persecuted by the colonial authorities and abandoned their efforts.

The new leadership that the Prophet Harris's converts found was of several varieties and led them in different directions. Yet all of the directions taken by his converts had been presaged in Harris' message and/or behavior. It is therefore not an exaggeration to say that all of the non-traditional religious institutions that presently exist in the southern Ivory Coast owe their origins, or their establishment in the area, to the influence of the Prophet Harris. The institutions in question encompass, in different kinds of ways, the Catholic Church, the Protestant Church, the Harrist Church, and the numerous other more or less successful original religious movements inspired by the Prophet.

Harris told the tens of thousands of people he baptized to go to church, and most of the churches available, with the exception of the few Methodist churches attended by the English-speaking clerks, were Catholic. The number of people who sought membership in the Catholic Church grew by leaps and bounds; it was far beyond the capacity of the few missionaries present to minister to this multitude of people whom they had been unable to attract on their own.

Many people, however, lived where there was no Catholic Church, or, finding no Bible in evidence in the Catholic Church they visited, concluded that Harris would not want them to go there because of the absence of the book containing the truth of his god. These people built their own churches and worshipped on their own under the leadership of a minister and apostles whom they designated. In the period after Harris's expulsion, the colonial administration decided to suppress such indigenous religious autonomy by arresting disciples and village leaders and destroying the churches or turning the finer structures over to the Catholic missionaries. Many people began to worship clandestinely while awaiting new religious leadership.

When the Protestant missionaries arrived in 1924, and were enthusiastically welcomed by village after village of "Harrist Protestants" as the "teachers with Bibles," they were immediately overwhelmed by people seeking to join their churches. Anxious to learn more about the man who had created this situation, the Protestant missionaries sent one of their number, the Reverend Pierre Benoit, to Liberia to find the Prophet Harris. Benoit found Harris and told him of the efforts of the Protestant missionaries to gather his converts into their churches. Harris, pleased that someone was picking up where he had left off, gave Benoit a "will" to all of his converts, telling them that it was his wish that they join the Methodist Church. On the basis of this will, the Protestants legitimated themselves in the eyes of many of Harris's converts as the Prophet's successors. The missionaries considered the Prophet to have been a kind of John the Baptist, whom God had sent to pave the way for them. The Methodist Church of the Ivory Coast presently dates its time of arrival in the Ivory Coast to the year 1914, which was the period of the Harrist movement, rather than 1924 when the first Prostestant missionaries actually arrived. They refer to the intervening decade as the "10 years of waiting," for themselves. The Protestant churches in some villages have signs saying "Methodist Mission, Founded by William Wade Harris," and the present head of the Methodist Church, whose parents were both baptized by Harris, said, "In a sense all Ivorian Christians, especially the Prostestants, are Harrists, because the

Prophet Harris was responsible for converting the first Christians." This is only a very slight exaggeration in that at the time when Harris arrived the only Ivorian Christians were the few hundred converted by the Catholics.

The Protestants also got a boost in the eastern part of the Ivory Coast and across the border into the Gold Coast from a man whom Harris had made a disciple, and who designated himself as the "Bishop of Sanwi." John Swatson was a Methodist agent from the Gold Coast working in the Ivory Coast when he encountered, and was favorably impressed by, the Prophet Harris in 1914. After being made a disciple by the Prophet, Swatson began to baptize people from both sides of the border and to send them to the Anglican Church in the Gold Coast, which welcomed his converts, accepted his baptism as valid, and even allowed polygamists to join the church (Haliburton 1971: 147–148).

After Benoit's visit to Harris, "Harrist Protestants" flocked to the Methodist mission churches in the Ivory Coast in even greater numbers because they believed that such was the Prophet's desire. A Protestant missionary in the Gold Coast said that the Prophet Harris had provided them with a tremendous, but embarrassing, opportunity because he had provided them with so many potential members whom their numbers were insufficient to accommodate.

However, some of the people who had been worshipping autonomously prior to the arrival of the Protestants resented ceding their authority to foreign missionaries, particularly when these latter condemned fundamental social institutions such as polygamy, requested financial support for the church, which looked suspiciously similar to the head tax demanded by the colonial authorities, and did not worship in the style that Harris had taught. With Harris they had worshipped the new god similarly to the way in which they had the old, with dancing and singing, and Harris had told them to sing their own songs, adding God's name. Such was not the case with the missionaries, who translated hymns from an alien musical tradition into the local languages and worshipped in a foreign and sober style that contrasted radically with that of the "Harrist Protestants."

Because of their discontent with this situation, a small delegation from the Ebrié village of Petit-Bassam went to Liberia in 1928 to see the Prophet and to tell him of their disappointment with the Protestant missionaries. They sought the Prophet's opinion on their areas of disagreement with the missionaries, hoping for his approval of their desire to continue worshipping autonomously. The delegation returned with Harris's approval of their decision to worship independently of the missionaries in their own style, and to conserve most aspects of their traditional social organization, including the institution of polygamy. The Prophet gave to John Ahui, a member of the delegation, a Bible and a cane cross like his own as a symbol of the transmittal of his spiritual legacy, and charged Ahui with the task of continuing his mission.

After returning home, John Ahui, attired like the Prophet and assisted by the two other Ebrié men who had been leading the religious life of their villages, set out to continue Harris's work of conversion to Christianity and to encourage those people who had been baptized by Harris and who had not joined a missionary church, to continue to worship as Harris had taught. For the people who came under the influence of John Ahui, their style of being Christian was based on a combination of Harris's teachings as gotten directly from the Prophet or from Ahui's interpretations, as well as on what they had gleaned about Christianity from the different disciples and missionaries with whom they had had contact, all understood in terms of their own indigenous belief system and social concerns. Where Harris had made no pronouncements, traditional modes prevailed, and elements of his teachings were given somewhat different meanings and interpretations than he had actually indicated in accordance with specific local social practices and concerns.

John Ahui's movement of conversion and consolidation, which encompassed the entire lagoons area, grew slowly during the 1930s because of opposition and oppression by the colonial administration. However, during the nationalist period of the 1940s, many people chose to reject the European missionary churches to which they belonged, especially the Catholic Church, in favor of what they called the "religion of the Africans." Harrist churches sprang up all over the lagoons area in villages in which the initial impetus dated from up to three decades earlier. Although these churches had developed independently of each other, among different ethnic groups, and with sometimes conflicting ideas, John Ahui managed to unite most of them under his leadership during the late 1940s and early 1950s, despite some struggles for control.

In the Grand Lahou area the Prophet Harris had had a particularly strong effect, and a number of disciples had continued his work. In that area 10 churches built as a result of Harris's initial impetus had avoided missionary control and remained autonomous for decades with no central authority. They had good rapport with the Protestant missionaries, from whom some members had learned to read the Bible (Amos-Djoro 1956: 3, 197). In the 1940s a conflict developed between these independent Harrist Churches of Grand Lahou and the expanding Harrist Church of John Ahui. The Grand Lahou group was united in 1949 by Gaston N'Drin, a church leader for the past 15 years, and refused the domination of the group led by John Ahui (Barrett 1968: 285; Bureau 1971: 40).

Another rival Harrist Church had been established close to N'Drin's church. Both its leader, Denis Abouré, and Gaston N'Drin insisted that they were practicing the true religion of the Prophet Harris. Both said that they had been delegated by the Prophet Harris himself and N'Drin maintained that he had received a cane cross from the Prophet Harris as a symbol of his right to continue the Prophet's mission. Seeking support for his position, Abouré summoned John Ahui to Grand Lahou. Ahui assembled a crowd of people of differing religious persuasions. Reminding them that he was Harris's true student and legitimate successor, he said that people were getting away from the Prophet's teachings. They were not respecting his laws and were committing too many sins. The way to return to the correct path was to unite under his own leadership. Ahui's argument persuaded much of his audience (Holas 1965: 288-290).

The major basis of doctrinal contention between Ahui's church and the Grand Lahou Harrists centered around the reading of the Bible. The Grand Lahou group placed great importance on the reading of the Bible because Harris had said that it contained the Word of God. John Ahui's group did not read the Bible. According to Holas, when N'Drin confronted Ahui on this point, saying that he had heard that Ahui prohibited Bible reading during services and urged parents not to send their children to school, Ahui replied that he personally did not read the Bible because he was not literate but that he did not prohibit others from reading it (Holas 1965: 290).

The basis of this issue lay in the difference in the relationship between the two Harrist groups and the Protestant missionaries. In contrast to the Grand Lahou group's good rapport with the missionaries, John Ahui's group had developed in direct opposition to them. Many of the schools that were set up in the colony were missionary schools and the children who went to the schools received religious training and were expected to become members of the church. Consequently, sending Harrist children to school usually resulted in their growing up to be Protestant or Catholic. In addition, with increased education they began to challenge the authority of their elders. However, John Ahui did send his own children to school, even sending them to stay with non-Harrist relatives in villages in which there were schools. Regarding the issue of reading the Bible, it has been suggested that Ahui opposed the reading of the Bible because it reflected a Protestant influence and obscured the true teachings of Harris. In actuality, the issue seems to have really been a non-issue since most church members were not literate. These problems have all been resolved. Harrist children go to government schools, the Bible is now read in church, and the Grand Lahou church has become affiliated with John Ahui's Harrist Church. Some leaders from Grand Lahou have become leaders in the larger Harrist Church structure.

The Harrist Church of the Ivory Coast has been officially recognized by the government as one of the four national religious institutions of the country, along with Protestantism, Catholicism, and Islam. It is the most important of the original religious forms that developed out of the teaching of the Prophet Harris in terms of numbers of members, external recognition, and relationship to the larger society. Its members consider it to be the only orthodox perpetuation of Harris's teaching in that it is a Christian church, similar to the Protestant church in many ways, but adapted to its African milieu in social organization, doctrinal content, and ritual style. In a national population of 5 million people the available religious statistics estimate that there are 100,000 Harrists, 200,000 Protestants, 500,000 Catholics, 1,000,000 Muslims. The majority of the population continues to practice the traditional religions.

THE HARRIST CHURCH

Most of the Harrist Churches are located in the Ebrié villages around Abidjan, capital of Ivory Coast. The church social organization reflects a combination of Harris's teachings and the indigenous social system. It is based essentially on the traditional age-grade structure, but also includes the added element of a group of apostles, because Harris told his converts to choose a minister and apostles to help him administer the church. Each church has an average of three ministers, depending upon the size of the congregation, and a group of apostles who ideally number 12, but in reality may be more or less, again depending upon congregation size. The apostles tend to be middle-aged men, the age-grade that has traditionally administered village life. There are two other status groups, not mentioned by Harris, whose structural positions follow the age-grade structure: the elders who as members of the oldest age-grade act as advisors to the ministers and apostles; and the choir, an important group composed of young men.

The older church buildings were built according to a simple, rather austere Protestant model, although the newer ones are very original in style, and church services are generally patterned after those of the Protestants. The service begins and ends with a procession from the chief minister's home to the church and back, the white-clad church members led by the ministers who are dressed in the style of the Prophet Harris. Going to church people just sing quiet songs, whereas returning from church they dance animatedly to more lively songs rhythmed by gourd rattles like the one the Prophet carried. The rattles are believed to carry the congregation's words to God, and the songs are thought to have an effect on the singers' consciences, encouraging them to behave properly.

The service consists of a sermon by the presiding minister relating biblical themes to local everday concerns, prayers by the minister and by him in conjunction with the congregation, numerous songs, some accompanied by the rattles, and benedictions. When a person receives a benediction he or she kneels before the minister, who places the Bible on the individual's head and says a prayer, — like a streamlined form of Harris's baptism. People request benedictions when they would like God's assistance in an undertaking, as they used to request the help of their traditional gods, and when they want to ask His forgiveness for sin. The church doctrine includes, in addition to the usual Ten Commandments, most of which already had analogues with commensurate sanctions in the indigenous social system, two additional commandments, which are seen as the most crucial. One prohibits having sexual relations out-of-doors, and the other forbids "eating human flesh and drinking human blood."

The first new commandment continues the traditional prohibition against defiling the earth in which the ancestors reside. The offended ancestors might provoke calamities such as droughts or epidemics for the entire village. The act is now explained, however, as an offense to God, for which He will punish the individuals concerned, because in having sexual relations out-of-doors, people are acting like animals rather than like humans.

The other prohibition is a metaphor for the practice of witchcraft, in which one person's soul is said to "eat" that of another. Because of this metaphor there is no communion, no eating of the flesh and drinking of the blood of Jesus. The concept of witchcraft provides the explanation for seemingly unprovoked and unmerited misfortune. Witchcraft is a major sin, punishable by God with illness. The guilty party must confess publicly in order to be cured. There are less serious prohibitions, like those against working on the Sabbath and eating meat on Fridays, and of course Harrists are strictly forbidden to use any religious objects from the indigenous religions on pain of punishment by God.

John Ahui, the church patriarch, continues to convert people and provide instruction for new ministers. He is aided by a corps of "ministers with canes." These men are carefully selected according to their superior moral qualities and knowledge about the church to assist Ahui in converting people. They carry cane crosses like Harris's as a symbol of their mission, using them to baptize people and to drive away evil spirits. The cross is an essential accoutrement found in every church. It must be erected at a special midnight ceremony at the beginning of which the ministers, who are the only people permitted to attend, must confess all of their transgressions. It is believed that people cannot harbor evil thoughts when in the presence of the cross in the church.

Since the mid-1950s the Harrists have been trying to elaborate a standard doctrine and liturgy and to improve their organizational structure for greater cohesion and uniformity among Harrist Churches. A first conference was held in 1955 to begin to resolve these issues. At that time a national structure was suggested, church holidays were designated, and the idea of setting up a youth organization to make young people a vital part of the church was proposed. Also a booklet of Harrist doctrine was written as a basis for the religious education of church members. Delegates at the conference decided that the Harrists should build a school as a visible expression of their commitment to educating their children as Harris had told them to do. This was done and the school was presented to the government. It is now part of the public school system. In 1964 a national committee was established to regulate church affairs and to handle relationships with other institutions including the government. In 1972 a youth conference sponsored by the national committee took place at which young literate church members discussed the modifications that they felt would be necessary for the church to become a more modern institution. It was proposed that the church begin to assume some secular functions such as contributing to the education and training of young members and setting up cooperative economic enterprises to generate capital for church projects.

The Harrist Church is trying to modernize to fit into contemporary Ivorian society. Although essentially a village phenomenon, the proximity of many Harrist Churches to urban areas, especially to the very modern national capital, has meant that they are quite influenced by the forces of change. Whereas the church was once characterized as a "religion of old men," its leaders are now trying to increase and assure its dynamism by getting young educated members more involved, to keep them from leaving it for the Catholic or Protestant Churches that are associated with social mobility. The Harrist Church is still growing by conversion as ministers continue to proselytize in non-Christianized areas. As an indication of how far the Harrist Church has come from the days in which the Prophet Harris, and later John Ahui, pursued their mission on foot, in 1971 John Ahui was presented with a Mercedes Benz by church members to facilitate his task of spreading his message throughout the country.

In the later discussion of the other original religious movements influenced by the Prophet Harris it will be immediately evident that an important feature in all of them is healing, particularly of illnesses caused by witchcraft, and trying to eliminate the practice of witchcraft altogether. It is only in the Harrist Church that this function is not the major ritual focus. People do confess their sins to the apostles and ministers and publicly request benedictions in church whether because of their sins, to assist them in an undertaking, or to thank God for something. Within the church there is concern with the eradication of witchcraft and its effects, but such is not the exclusive or principal preoccupation of the church, which has broader concerns. However, there is a branch of the Harrist Church which functions similarly to the movements that are mainly dedicated to healing and to eliminating witchcraft. This branch is localized in the village of Bregbo under the leadership of Albert Atcho, who has become known all along the coastal area for his healing activities.

Albert Atcho is from a family of herbal doctors and has been healing since the 1920s. He joined the Harrist Church in the 1940s and played an important role in helping John Ahui extend its influence. Atcho's renown as a healer has brought many new members to the church. People of all religious persuasions, Protestant, Catholic, Muslim, Harrist, and traditionalist, go to him. A great many of those whom he heals decide that it would be beneficial to join the church of the person who has healed them. In addition to being the Church's official healer, Atcho has an important administrative role. Since 1967 he has been the chairman of the national committee that determines church policy.

People visit Atcho when they find themselves ill, and when church benedictions or the care of local healers do not help. When a sick person arrives in Bregbo, one of Atcho's assistants notes the nature of the illness in a notebook. When the person comes before Atcho for treatment, the healer diagnoses his or her case, and the patient must make a full public confession of all sins before he or she can be cured. Most of the people who come to Atcho are the victims or the perpetrators of witchcraft, usually the latter. After making a complete confession, they are given a mixture of herbs and water to drink and with which to wash. People take away bottles of water blessed by Atcho, and also bring bottles of cologne and boxes of talcum powder for him to bless for use for protective purposes. Atcho explains that his power comes from God and that he asks God to heal the person. God will not do so if the person tries to hide any sins.

Some of the people who see Atcho only come to Bregbo for his healing sessions. Others who are more seriously ill stay for periods of varying lengths of time in the village. They bring members of their families and build a house or move into an empty one. Well members of the family participate in village economic activities that benefit the collectivity. Many people who have been healed by Atcho prefer to stay on rather than to return home because in Bregbo they feel that they live under the healer's protection. Consequently, Bregbo has grown from a handful of people to a large village of more than 1000 inhabitants. A nearby mental institution has recognized Atcho's success in treating many patients, and hospital and healer sometimes combine their modern Western and indigenous traditional techniques to treat people.

Thus, because of Albert Atcho the healing function that is central in most of the Harrist-inspired groups exists as a component of the Harrist Church, but it is in a sense a separate branch, and not for Harrists only, since after being healed one need not necessarily join the church, although many people do. Since the Prophet Harris's verbal message was like that of the missionaries and his behavioral one like that of the traditional priests, John Ahui, who established the church and converts people to Christianity, and Albert Atcho, who heals people and fights against witchcraft, may be seen respectively to personify these two trends as combined in the Harrist Church.

THE POLYVALENT MESSAGE

How can one account for the phenomenal appeal exercised by the Prophet Harris that allowed him to revolutionize the religious lives of more than 100,000 people in the largest multiethnic mass movement in the Ivory Coast prior to the nationalist movement of the 1940's? Max Weber emphasizes the role of the charismatic prophet as the ideal change agent in promoting a radical breakthrough from one religious system to another. The appeal of this charismatic prophet is based on authoritativeness derived from an ultimate source that allows his message to compel the allegiance of masses of people in opposition to the traditional order. Under the influence of this prophetic figure people come together in a movement based on their allegiance to the prophet because of the new meanings and techniques for salvation that he offers them. According to Weber's formulation, the movement phase is only a temporary phenomenon, which, if it is to develop into a permanent institution, must be routinized by the sharing or transmission of the original charisma of the prophet to another person or persons. The new leader or leaders will function as (a) perpetuator(s) of the movement by developing it into an organizational and doctrinal framework based on the prophet's message and activities (Weber 1947: 358-359).

The Prophet Harris fits Weber's characterization of the charismatic prophet very well both as a person and in his accomplishments. Described as a very impressive figure with a particularly fervent preaching style, Harris was perceived by his audiences as different from other people, and his effect stood outside the routines of everyday life. He was seen as a son of God or as an extremely powerful traditional priest with a compelling message. His influence caused people to break with the traditional religious order and seek to direct their religious life in new directions. The Harrist Church was developed to institutionalize a way to perpetuate the Prophet Harris's influence. Some of the Prophet Harris's personal charisma may be considered to have been transmitted to John Ahui, founder and head of the church, with the symbols of his mission — the cane cross and the Bible — that Harris gave him. Ahui is believed by Harrists to have continued Harris' work in the same style the Prophet had used, and to Ahui are attributed the same types of miracles that Harris was said to have performed. Church members obscure the difference between the roles of the two men — the charismatic innovator and the secular organizer — by sometimes referring to both of them as "prophet."

Worsley raises fundamental objections to Weber's formulation of the concept of charisma, the basis of which lies in Weber's perception of charisma as "a certain quality of an individual personality" (Weber 1947: 358). Worsley emphasizes the fact that the appeal of an individual labeled as charismatic is multifaceted, being composed of his acts and his messages in addition to his personal attributes. For Worsley what is significant is less the nature of the personality or acts of the individual than the fact that in order for the person's appeal to provide a basis for social action, it must be perceived as meaningful and be acted upon by his audience. Hence the concept of charisma defines for Worsley not the personal characteristics of an outstanding individual, but the social relationship established between the individual and his audience, which is a function of their recognition of him as embodying values in which they have an interest. He claims to be able to actualize those values, and must be able to furnish sufficiently convincing proof to that effect if he is to be successful. The factor in the potential leader's appeal that creates the basis for the social relationship, which is therefore the actual basis of the charismatic rapport, is the message. The message must appeal to the values of the audience, manifesting shared fundamental assumptions between the leader and the followers, speaking to the followers' unsatisfied wants, and promising their eventual fulfillment (Worsley 1968: x–xiv).

Worsley's model of the concept of charismatic authority is interactional rather than unidirectional, and the message is the most important element. Worsley notes that the person of the prophet is unimportant in some charismatic movements. A leader is created to embody the desires of the followers, and the prophet merely transmits a message that he has not created. When the message is much more important than the person of the leader there is a greater tendency for facets of the movement to diverge in different directions under a variety of new leaders. Other leaders do define their messages, and their definitions become gospel for the movement. In either case the most significant factor is the social significance of the leader as a message bearer and a symbolizer of something new to his followers. They, in turn, must invest him with authority by their acceptance, and as a result of his stimulus, create an organization embodying his innovations (Worsley 1968: xiv–xviii).

Worsley's emphasis on the relational nature of charisma and on the essentiality of the message in providing the linkage and basis for the relationship between the leader and the followers makes for greater explanatory clarity, improving on Weber's formulation. Worsley's approach can explain situations in which the same individual, with the same divine revelation, forceful personality, and style of presentation, is phenomenally successful in one place and has absolutely no effect in others. It does so by focusing on the role of the audience in establishing a leader as charismatic by their approval of a message that strikes a responsive chord, or of withholding this approval if his message says nothing to them.

It is undeniable, for example, that the Prophet Harris cut a very impressive figure for a large portion of the population of the southern Ivory Coast. In addition to his visual presentation as a physically impressive man dressed in unique garb and carrying novel religious accoutrements, he was described by early chroniclers as preaching in a booming voice in a fervent and fiery manner. It is also undeniable, however, that these same personal characteristics, coupled with the same message of his divine revelation, met with rejection in his native Liberia, where he was viewed as an eccentric, not as God's last prophet. In the Ivory Coast conditions were such as to make people receptive to a new message since many aspects of their traditional way of life were being put into question by the colonial impact. However, there also, in spite of Harris's personal appeal, his message only began to be considered really relevant, and he only began to be regarded as a source of authority, when he gave proof of the validity of some of his contentions. Only then was his audience given a basis for believing that the new definitions and techniques he proposed indeed held the promise of allowing them to realize the values that his message contained. He also embodied and symbolized for them the attainment of these values, in himself furnishing the proof that such was possible for an African like themselves.

The emphasis on the centrality of the message and the nature of the understandings and interests of the audience in the creation of a charismatic movement is particularly pertinent to a discussion of the Harrist churches of the Ivory Coast. As has been noted, the influence of the Prophet Harris was at the origin of the growth of the Catholic Church and the establishment of the Protestant Church as well as the creation of the Harrist Church in the Ivory Coast. The reason for which these three different developments resulted from Harris's activities was the fact that his message meant different things to different groups of people, all of whom accorded him the authority necessary to encourage them to follow a new path traced out for them by him.

In addition to provoking the growth or establishment of the two missionary churches and the development of a third Christian religious institution based on indigenous African values, the Prophet Harris was also at the origin of the development of several other innovative religious movements in the country. After he was repatriated his converts sought leaders who would guide them in how to practice the new religion begun by Harris now that they had given up the old one. They knew quite a bit about what they were not to do, but had many questions about what they were to do. The Catholic missionaries could not accommodate everyone, nor did they appeal to all the Prophet's converts. Others sought assistance from Harris's disciples to guide them in their worship under their own appointed leaders. Still others worshipped entirely on their own.

The Christianity of the latter was based on what they had gleaned from Harris's teachings when he came to their villages or from what a village delegate who had gone to see the Prophet had retained. Some of the clerk-disciples continued to travel around to spread Harris's message inland, and Victor Nivri drew people to himself to be baptized. His village of Addah became a center of pilgrimage. He wore a white robe and hat and also traveled around baptizing. In some places new "prophets" sprang up with novel schemes, and in some villages people made religious changes based on rumors they had heard about the Prophet Harris. With the Prophet Harris no longer present as a basis for authentication, those designated by Harris or self-designated as religious leaders exercised a great deal of freedom in determining the religious orientation of those who chose to follow them.

Harris's actual message lent itself to different interpretations, and when transmitted by different leaders to groups of differing orientations it acquired further variations. For example, some of the coastal people, who were beginnning to experience new prosperity as a result of the colonial situation, were encouraged by Harris's influence to work diligently and obey the colonial authorities. Some inland groups, however, who remained hostile to the French, received a transformed version of Harris's message, or understood his message in a way transformed by their own orientation, saying that the son of God was going to get rid of the French so that the Africans could regain their sovereignty and return to a more pleasant way of life. Therefore, rather than seeing obedience to the colonial authorities as serving their own interests, they increased their defiance of those they saw as the soon to be defeated colonial officials.

The three groups who became Catholics, Protestants, and Harrists each justified their choice on the basis of some aspects of the Prophet Harris's verbal or behavioral message. Those who became Catholic did so on the basis that Harris had told them to go to the existing churches, which were at that time Catholic, and that he even accompanied groups of people to Catholic churches. Those people who became Protestant did so on the basis of three factors. The Prophet had himself been a Protestant—although speaking to the head of the Catholic mission he said that he was above all religions—as were the clerk-disciples who provided his immediate follow-up. It is for this reason that this group called themselves "Harrist Protestants" before the arrival of the missionaries. Second, Harris had told many of his converts that "teachers with Bibles" would come along to show them how to be Christians. When the Protestant missionaries arrived they were believed to be the teachers with Bibles whose arrival Harris had predicted. The third reason was the Prophet's "will" brought back from Liberia by Reverend Benoit. The will had the effect desired by the Protestants of convincing many people that the Prophet's desire was that they join the Protestant Church.

The justification for developing and belonging to the Harrist Church comes not only from Harris's verbal message but also from his behavioral message, the cues of which counterbalanced some aspects of his verbal message. It was the ambiguities represented by the difference between Harris's verbal and behavioral messages, in interaction with the orientations of the different recipients of these messages, that accounted for the development both of the Harrist Church and of the other churches that claim him as their founder. The fact that differing religious orientations developed as a result of his activities is not a result of his lack of importance as a leader, a possibility suggested by Worsley. That he was no longer physically present was, of course, significant because he could not act as the ultimate arbiter of what was right. In fact, when consulted in Liberia he gave his approval of two different possibilities—that his converts should join the Protestant Church and that they should worship on their own. The significant fact, however, is that his message was sufficiently general and fundamental that people could legitimately respond to his central preoccupation in a number of different ways. He wanted them to be Christians. The style of Christianity they adopted was of secondary concern to him.

Because he had role attributes from two different cultural orientations, that of the traditional priest introducing a new and stronger deity and that of the European missionary bringing Christianity, Harris was perceived by some people as a great traditional priest and by others as a son of God. His different audiences' varied perceptions of him and understandings of the meaning of his mission determined that the religious activities that resulted would differ in orientation. Moreover, the fact that his verbal cues associated him with one cultural tradition and his behavorial cues with another allowed his audiences much leeway in deciding which aspects of his message to regard as central and to elaborate in their own institutions.

The Harris Church had its origins when people who had originally welcomed the teachers with Bibles began to question the validity of the statement in the Prophet Harris's will that all of his converts should become Protestant. In addition to resenting the Protestants' requests for money and their attack on the indigenous social organization, which departed from the Prophet's practice, the Ivorians found the missionaries' worship style unacceptable because it did not correspond to Harris's behavioral message, which provided their model of Christian worship. The Prophet had told them, for example, to sing for the new god as they had for the old ones, which was not what took place in Protestant ceremonies. In addition, there was no role in the Protestant church for the apostles whom Harris had said should run the church. Many of the people who had originally heeded Harris's verbal message to go to the already present Catholic churches left when they did not find a Bible present. The Bible formed a very important part of Harris's behavioral message since he used it both for preaching God's words and for baptizing.

When the Harrist Church was developed, its ritual style was patterned to mirror the Prophet's. The ministers wear outfits like his; the processions to and from the church reenact the welcoming gesture of the people to whose villages he went who, once he was well known, waited for him at the entrance to the village to accompany him to the center and then accompanied him back after he had addressed them; many songs are sung during the worship service; and the Bible, the cross, the baptismal gourd, and the gourd rattle play important roles. All this is in response to the Prophet's behavorial rather than verbal message.

The Protestants assert that the Harrists did not understand or heed the Prophet's true desire for his converts, which was to join the Protestant Church. The Harrists retort that Harris only wanted them to join the Protestant Church on the assumption that the missionaries would worship as he had taught. Learning that the missionaries were not doing so, he told the Ivorian delegation that he preferred that his converts worship on their own, following the model he had set for them. Thus, the members of each of the three churches selected different facets of Harris's message to elaborate in justification of their choice. The individuals who developed entirely new religious movements selected still other elements of his message to elaborate. Although divine revelation led many of them to their calling, most of these new prophets and prophetesses claimed to be successors to the Prophet Harris in some way, and all of their movements reflect the clear imprint of his influence.

THE OTHER HARRIST CHURCHES

The Church of the Twelve Apostles

The first new religious movement that developed to continue the Prophet Harris's work was in the southwestern Gold Coast in the Nzima area. Grace Thannie, a woman whom Harris had baptized there, and who had been a traditional priestess whose spirit he had driven away, joined his entourage and accompanied him and his two Liberian companions back to the Ivory Coast. When the Liberians were repatriated she returned home. Calling herself Madame Harris Grace Thannie, she became the leader of many people Harris had baptized in her area. She and her followers, calling themselves prophets and prophetesses, dressed in white and sang to the accompaniment of gourd rattles hymns Harris had taught them. Their aim was mainly to exorcise evil spirits as Harris had done when people possessed by them touched his cane cross to rid themselves of them and were subsequently baptized. This to them was the meaningful part of Harris's activities. The multiethnic church Thannie founded was called "The Church of William Wade Harris and his Twelve Apostles." The prophets and prophetesses supposedly performed miraculous cures because of their faith in God (Haliburton 1971: 148-149). More commonly known as the "Church of the Twelve Apostles," Thannie's church lays claim to being the first "spiritualist church" in the country. The term spiritualist church in the Ghanaian context designates those religious institutions that in their worship, "engage in activities that are meant to invoke the Holy Spirit of God, or to be interpreted as signs of his descent upon the worshippers" (Baëta 1962: 1, 8, 9).

Named the Church of the Twelve Apostles because of the 12 apostles Harris had told people to choose to administer their churches, the church's present organization does not follow that original intent. Each local prophet or prophetess is autonomous and claims the inspiration of the "spirit" to do as he or she wishes. There are no apostles and there is no central organization. There are district leaders who are relatively independent of each other yet church practice is, nevertheless, quite standard. Most leaders are not literate, but in the future, new leaders must be literate, at least in an African language, and one educated member undertook to write a catechism, a hymn book, and a service book in the Fanti language (Baëta 1962: 9-14).

A person desirous of becoming a prophet or prophetess goes to the "garden" of an established prophet or prophetess to ascertain whether or not he or she has the aptitude and calling, and if so remains to observe what the prophet or prophetess does. Although church leaders claim to subscribe to the same doctrine as the Methodists, Baëta states that no doctrine is actually taught in the Church of the Twelve Apostles. Emphasis is on the activity of the Holy Spirit in enabling qualified individuals to predict future events, warn of impending misfortune, detect evildoers, and especially to heal people from illness. As one member said of their main concern, "We are here to heal" (Baëta 1962: 12, 15).

The garden is the center of religious activities, and each prophet or prophetess has one. It has a number of living compartments for patients in residence, who may number from 10 to 30. Other patients come by appointment. In the center of the garden stands a tall wooden cross. Every morning, and on other occasions when more holy water is needed, a basin of water is raised before the cross three times with a prayer that it be blessed by the Holy Spirit. It may be used at once for healing or it may be stored at the foot of the cross for future use. Healing is attributed to the effect of the holy water in conjunction with the patient's faith. The Holy Spirit decides if a cure is possible and so informs the prophet. The patients carry a pan of the holy water on their heads and begin to dance around the garden to musical accompaniment. As the music gets louder the spirit enters the patients, who dance harder until the water spills on their bodies. After they have danced, the remaining water is kept by the patients to serve as personal medicine (Baëta 1962: 19-21).

In the reception area of the garden there are worship services every morning and Tuesday and Thursday evenings. There is little teaching, but there are many prayers accompanied by ecstatic shouts, which often end in songs. The theme of the prayers tends to be healing. The members of the church criticize the mission churches for not healing, citing the fact that since Jesus Christ healed in the Bible the reason for which the missionaries do not heal lies in their inability due to their insufficient faith (Baëta 1962: 19-21, 137).

In addition to the cross, the Bible and the gourd rattle are also sacred objects. An English Bible is always prominently displayed at prayer and healing meetings. It is not read but is touched to the head of the person to be baptized or healed. The gourd rattle is an indispensable accoutrement of the prophets and prophetesses as well as of the singers. When posing for official photographs, the prophets and prophetesses don white robes and hats, holding a Bible and rattle in the left hand and a cane cross in the right, so that they look just like the photographs of the Prophet Harris (Baëta 1962: 16–18).

Many regular members also possess rattles. They are made by women and are thought to be effective in chasing away evil spirits and in healing. At one point the Church of the Twelve Apostles considered affiliating with an American Pentecostal Church with a branch in Accra, capital of Ghana, from which they expected leadership and financial assistance. The Pentecostal missionaries who came to consider their request approved of their affiliating but demanded that they substitute tambourines for the rattles. The leaders of the Church of the Twelve Apostles were alarmed because the rattles chase away evil spirits whereas the tambourines just make noise. They requested to be allowed to keep their rattles and, when refused permisssion, decided against the new affiliation because they felt that the foreign missionaries were trying to deprive them of their spiritual power. A picture in one church depicts Moses striking a rock to obtain water in the wilderness. The water pots carried by the women in the picture have the same form as the gourd rattles. The picture is cited to prove the importance of the rattles in all worship services if the prayers of the congregation are to be transmitted to God without being distorted or made ineffective by evil spirits (Baëta 1962: 16–18).

Admission to the church is through baptism. The person is bathed and scrubbed all over by someone of the same sex, and then the sign of the cross is made over him or her. The person receives no religious instruction but is expected to participate in church activities. There is a love feast once a year at which members share bread and hear a discourse on brotherhood and unity. Once or twice a year the head of each district celebrates communion. At this time there are public confessions of sins followed by the sharing of bread and wine blessed by the leader (Baëta 1962: 18).

The leaders of the Church of the Twelve Apostles claim the Prophet Harris's authority for everything they do, although it is apparent that their present practices were evolved by their own leaders. There is actually little emphasis on Harris's teaching in the organization or rules of behavior except for the absolute prohibition of the use of traditional religious objects. The focus on healing did not come from the Prophet. Harris is credited with some healing, but neither accounts of his words and activities written at the time of the movement nor the oral tradition emphasizes this aspect of his behavior. Had healing been more fundamental to the Prophet's behavior, one would expect it to be a central feature of the Harrist Church of the Ivory Coast.

The Church of Bodjo Aké

The first new prophet to develop a religious movement of some importance in the Ivory Coast was Bodjo Aké, an Alladian who was first mentioned in a political report in 1926 (Augé 1969: 186). Aké claimed to be a messenger of God, taking the places of both the Prophet Harris and of God Himself, unlike John Ahui who acknowledged Harris as God's only messenger and claimed only to be Harris's disciple. After Aké's death it was he, rather than God or Harris, who was addressed in prayers.

Services included preaching by his ministers and songs by the congregation. During the songs and while the ministers were preaching, members would go into trances and roll on the ground, manifesting the pleasure or displeasure of the spirits and angels. To calm them the preacher would touch the Bible to their heads and say a prayer in what was thought to be the English of the Prophet Harris, which no one understood (Amos-Djoro 1956: 271). Aké baptized with "water from heaven" and preached a doctrine like Harris's — forbidding killing, theft, adultery, working on Sunday, cursing one's neighbors, eating certain foods, and having sexual relations in the open air. He permitted polygamy (Yando 1970: 55; Amos-Djoro 1956: 279).

Aké vigorously opposed the Protestant missionaries for the same reasons as did John Ahui, and said that he had received a message from Harris to the effect that the missionaries had come to trick the Africans and steal their money (Yando 1970: 55). He and his followers came into conflict with Methodist authorities and with the Methodist members of some villages in which Aké had followers, often over use of a church building that had been built by all of the villagers prior to the coming of the Protestant missionaries and then turned over to the Methodists. When the Akéists also wanted to use the church there were sometimes physical struggles such as one in the village of Gamo in which the church was damaged and the bell taken by the group led by Aké (Haliburton 1971: 195–196). It was during this period of 1924–1926, when the newly arrived Methodists were trying to establish their authority, and partially as a result of such challenges to it, that the Protestants sent Reverend Benoit to see Harris to try to legitimate themselves by establishing a link with the Prophet.

Aké had his greatest influence in the inland part of the lagoons area around Dabou among the Adjoukrou, with some influence also among the Abidji and later among the Abbey. He had his largest following among those contingents of villagers for whom the missionary influence represented a diminishing of their own power. These were mainly the men in the forties to fifties age group who had been the undisputed village leaders, and who resented the young Protestant religious teachers from Togo and Dahomey who were sent to instruct them. The semiliterate or non-literate older men also objected to the fact that through the missionary schools the younger men of their village were able to acquire new knowledge with which to challenge their own previous status as undisputed village leaders. In some places people resisted Aké's influence or after having come under it, returned to the Methodist Church, believing that the Methodist missionaries were indeed the teachers with Bibles about whom Harris had talked (Amos-Djoro 1956: 266; Haliburton 1971: 197). The will brought back by Benoit served to convince them.

Obodji Soboa, chief of the Abbey people, favored the spread of Aké's version of Harris' Christianity to the Abbeys. He made the religion mandatory for all of his people with himself as the leader of the "Church of Obodji" or the "Religion of the King." There was a fine for those who resisted joining. Obodji had been Catholic but quarreled with the missionaries upon becoming chief, and he was scornful of the Protestants. Each church had a preacher who sacrificed to God animals which were then consumed by the villagers. Each Sunday there was a service with communion, and there were daily prayers. Members were not to engage in sexual relations before a service and had to confess any transgressions in this area to a preacher. Obodji had a sacred hill called Jerusalem to which church members went to be purified. Yearly ceremonies were held there to which people brought animals and money for God. They danced and spent two nights there. On the third day Obodji went to the top of the hill to get a message from God and came right down in ecstasy, gesturing that the ceremony was over. Aké died in 1931 and his cult lost most of its influence, although a man named Ambroise Esmer kept a spark alive among the Adjoukrou (Bureau 1971: 39). The cult died among the Abbeys with Chief Obodji Soboa and the members returned to the missionary churches (Amos-Djoro 1956: 267, 277–279).

The Church of Jonas Zaka

Another religious leader who began to oppose the Protestant missionaries was Jonas Zaka, an Ebrié from the village of Akuédo. The villagers of Akuédo had seen Harris at Jacqueville. Baptized by him, the

entire village fervently followed his teachings and enthusiastically received the Protestant teachers with Bibles at their arrival. The church
that they had built 10 years earlier at Harris' urging was given over to
the missionaries. The villagers resisted the influence of both John
Ahui and Bodjo Aké because they felt that they were correctly following Harris's teachings by becoming Protestant. A dynamic villager
named Jonas Zaka received religious instruction from the missionaries and became the minister. He used the Bible as his main guide,
and many villagers learned by heart some bibilical passages mainly
from the Old Testament (Amos-Djoro 1956: 300, 302-303).

After several years Zaka lost his zeal for the mission church,
considering that the missionaries wanted to use the church more for
social than for religious ends. He became discontented with the disciplinary measures taken by the missionaries against those church
members who violated the social restrictions they imposed. A com-
plaint to the missionaries had no effect, so he and a group of dissidents left the church and founded their own in 1935. Zaka had little
success in his own village, which remained Methodist, but was very
successful in other nearby villages, although his movement never
achieved great geographic expansion. In the village of Dagbé, which
Harris had visited but in which people had not heeded his message,
one-half of them began to follow Zaka. In 1940 there were about
1000 members of the Zaka Church, which never got outside the
Ebrié area and lasted only until 1945 (Amos-Djoro 1956: 300).

Zaka was not violently opposed to the Protestant missionaries
but maintained good rapport with them. He claimed no special revelation for separating from the Methodists. He maintained, however,
that it was possible for Africans to obey the authority of the Bible
without belonging to a European church that made unreasonable
social demands on them. Zaka tried to distinguish his own religious
orientation both from the traditional religious influences and from
those of the missionaries. His church had a Bible school that provided both religious and social education, and there were social organizations for both women and young people. No stand was taken
on polygamy which was tantamount to approving of its continued
existence (Amos-Djoro 1956: 303-306).

Zaka vigorously opposed Bodjo Aké because the latter opposed
the use of the Bible, which Aké saw as a tool of the Protestants by
which they provided new knowledge to inspire the young to rebellion.
Zaka also opposed the Harrists of John Ahui, whom he considered
"fetishists." When the Zaka movement began to decline, the Seventh
Day Adventists, with the help of Zaka's son, tried to recruit its

members but they did not like Adventist rules such as the food restrictions or the fact that the Sabbath was on Saturday rather than
on Sunday. In spite of Zaka's earlier opposition, most of his former
followers became Harrists and were rebaptized by John Ahui (Amos-
Djoro 1956: 300, 304, 310).

Since they were Ebrié, Zaka's followers lived in the area in
which John Ahui was making his most concentrated efforts, and the
time of the decline of the Zaka Church corresponded with the beginning of Ahui's expansion. The Harrist Church began to expand so
rapidly at this time, during the nationalist period, because of its
status as a "religion of Africans" unassociated with the European
churches, and because it had the authority of being the direct legacy
of the Prophet Harris whom God had especially chosen to bring it to
the Ivorians. As the Harrist Church expanded it won converts not
only from the Protestant and Catholic Churches but also from other
sects inspired by Harris's teaching but lacking Ahui's direct legitimation by the Prophet Harris.

The Church of Bébéh Gra

Another movement, begun by Togbah or Bébéh Gra, came to
administrative attention in the Alladian area in 1932. This movement,
along with the Protestant Church, provided competition for Aké's efforts. Bébéh Gra did not claim to be a successor of the Prophet Harris, who had been less influential in the Sassandra area than in the lagoons area. He was more in the tradition of a traditional priest
(Amos-Djoro 1956: 265; Augé 1969: 196). However, his emphasis
on the fact that people were sinning by worshipping the traditional
deities rather than God suggests Harris' influence.

The explanation of Bébéh Gra's calling is as follows: One night
he was awakened by a luminous figure who said that everything was
wrong in the country. People no longer respected chiefs or elders
and young men took the wives of others, got drunk, and worshipped
fetishes. Bébéh Gra was to tell his brothers to cease such behavior.
The next morning he began haranguing his neighbors who, thinking
he had become insane, chained him up. God told him that He would
send a sign to convince the non-believers. Soon the villagers heard a
bell ring where there was none, but still they kept Bébéh Gra chained. Freeing himself he fled to the forest where he subsisted for 3
years, sometimes begging in markets. At the end of this time God
came to his rescue and he cleaned up and returned to his village where
people gathered around him to pray (Augé 1969: 186).

In about 1954 Dabri Njava, an Ebrié, came on the scene, absorbing most of Bébéh Gra's followers as well as those left from the Aké movement who had been led by Ambroise Esmer since Aké's death (Bureau 1971: 39; Yando 1970: 55). Some villages, such as the Aizi village of Tiagba, continue to have Bébéh churches. Tiagba is divided into three areas, Catholic, Protestant, and Bébéh. The Bébéh Church permits polygamy so has the largest families, but otherwise there is no difference in life-styles among members of the different churches. In the Bébéh Church there are processions and much singing and dancing (Bonnefoy 1954: 30, 45, 55).

The Church of Papa Nouveau

Dagri Njava, who became known as Papa Nouveau, claimed to be the successor of Bébéh Gra, and said he had no link with the Prophet Harris. According to his conversion story Papa Nouveau had a revelation while fishing near Jacqueville. People initially thought he was insane, but he finally won many followers. Believed to be associated with the traditional cult of the sea of the coastal Alladian, his power is thought by some to result from the fact that he is the husband of the powerful water goddess Mammy Wata (Augé 1969: 184-186, 195).

There are differences between the churches of Bébéh Gra and Papa Nouveau. The followers of the former danced until they were exhausted, some going into trances, whereas Papa Nouveau's services are more controlled. Friday is the holy day for both churches, just as it was for the cult of Mammy Wata, and a main concern of both churches is fertility, again suggesting the Mammy Wata cult. The Alladian wish to have a large population including many young men to work and they attribute sterility to witchcraft (Augé 1969: 184, 187). Bébéh Gra did not use the Bible, and a major concern of his was eliminating witchcraft. The same is true of Papa Nouveau (Bureau 1971: 39).

Although initially claiming no link with the Prophet Harris, Papa Nouveau has become more closely associated with the Harrists. Some Harrists resent the fact that Papa Nouveau's Church is seen as a Harrist sect by outsiders, who indiscriminately tend to lump religious manifestations not associated with the missionary churches with the Harrists. These Harrists say he is not a Harrist because his holy day is Friday, not Sunday, and because he claims personal inspiration to preach, rather than saying that he is a disciple of the Prophet Harris. Other Harrists feel that Papa Nouveau's church does indeed fit within the scope of their religion and accept what they consider minor liturgical variations.

Quite successful and prosperous, Papa Nouveau has a 3000-seat church in the village of Toukouzou, which he has rebaptized Hozalem, his version of Jerusalem. At present the Harrists, having become recognized by the government as an established religion, are trying to standardize their organization, doctrine, and practice with an eye to creating uniform criteria that all Harrist churches must meet and in order to make a clear distinction between themselves and other religious sects with which they might be confused. All those who would be Harrists must also recognize John Ahui as Harris's successor and as head of the church, which Papa Nouveau has not done.

Crastchotche

Another church that developed directly out of the Harrist movement is the "Eglise Crastchotche," in the Dida village of Ahouati, and all of the villagers belong to it. The church also has some members in other Dida villages as well as in some Alladian and Ebrié villages. When the Prophet Harris was in the Grand Lahou area the entire population of Ahouati went to see him. They all destroyed their traditional religious objects and were baptized by the Prophet. Harris is said to have told the people of Ahouati that they should be patient and soon they would not have to come so far to hear him because God would send them a messenger. When a man named Makoui appeared in the Divo area in 1935 claiming to be a prophet it was believed that he was this messenger (Bernus 1957: 217, 219; Holas 1965: 298).

Makoui preached in English and people did not know where he was from. He was, however, quite successful in getting people in a number of villages around the town of Divo to build churches. He said to call them "Christ Church," which became Crastchotche. The French administration arrested him and sent him to Abidjan to prison. Released, he sought refuge in an Ebrié village near Grand Bassam. Some of his Dida followers joined him there. They received further religious instruction from him and learned the songs in Ebrié that they still sing. Makoui had had time to designate some successors before leaving the Divo area. One successor initially converted and baptized people, but soon lost his zeal and joined the Protestant Church. Ahouati is the only village that has remained faithful to Prophet Makoui. Many of the people whom he had converted in other villages returned to their traditional religion or joined the Catholic, Protestant, or Harrist churches (Bernus 1957: 217, 219).

For the followers of Makoui the role of the Prophet Harris was to announce the coming of the Prophet Makoui, so Harris was but a messenger to foretell the arrival of a man sent by God. There are four ministers in the church because the man who initially succeeded Makoui designated four. The ministers, who each serve for a week at a time, are members of the apostles or elders, who do not number 12 and who direct the church. Other roles in the church are those of the bell ringers, who summon members to services, and the guardians who open the church and keep it neat and keep order among the congregation during the services. Life in the village is determined by the rhythm of church services. Sunday and Friday are both dedicated to the religious life, so the villagers do not work. People go into church barefoot and are supposed to wear different colored outfits on different days of the week. On Friday they should wear black for the death of Christ, on Tuesday and Wednesday, red for the blood spilled on the cross, and on Thursday and Sunday, white for the last Supper and the Resurrection. Each costume for church attendance is supposed to have a cross on the chest. In reality, most members do not have so many outfits, but wear clothes in which they have not worked (Bernus 1957: 218).

The preacher wears a miter and sits on a sort of throne lit by two candles with an altar before him with a cross upon it. The apostles sit around him, separated from the congregation by a guard rail. Preaching is in Dida, with prayers in a facsimile of English. One of the major prayers is the Lord's Prayer. Most songs are sung in Ebrié accompanied by the rhythm of gourd rattles (Bernus 1957: 219).

The Church of Boto Adai

Another Ivorian prophet whose movement was quite successful and achieved some geographic extension was Boto Adai. An Nzima from the Assinie region of the Ivory Coast, Adai had received rudimentary religious instruction from Protestant missionaries and had read some of the Bible. He had worked for the colonial administration and then left his home area for Grand Lahou where he began to transport and sell fish. Quite successful in that, he tried to set up an industrial-scale cocoa plantation. It failed, and as his financial state worsened he began to pray. He started a new plantation which he named Onza-Niamlé-yo or "Nothing can be done without the aid of God," after which his fate took a turn for the better to the point that he became very prosperous (Holas 1965: 72).

In 1932 Adai had a vision in which an angel told him that God had designated him as His minister on earth. He was to preach God's words and heal people who were of good faith. Frightened, Adai responded that he was a simple farmer incapable of accomplishing such a mission and asked how he would be able to support his family. He said that he felt that he was too weak to overcome, as the Prophet Harris had done, the obstacles he would encounter in trying to fulfill such a mission. Thereafter, Adai fell ill and had more visions of the angel telling him that he must fulfill the mission. Realizing that he had offended God he began to pray, promising to do His bidding. Upon getting well he moved to his plantation on the Boubo River and began his church. For this he was immediately excommunicated by the Methodist Church of which he had been a member and to which he still considered himself loyal (Holas 1965: 70–76).

Although some people gathered in his new community, Adai was not yet settled into his new role and spent most of his time meditating and comforting, but not healing, sick people. The turning point came in 1935 when on a visit to an Nzima village he was present when two local healers failed to heal a man who was close to death. Adai asked the man's parents for water and rice powder, which he blessed. He talked to the man, had him drink the water, and coated his face with the powder. The next day the man was well. This event marked the confirmation of Adai's power that gave him the confidence to take up his mission. It also established his reputation and gained him many followers. The number of his followers grew and his church spread to many villages among his own Nzima people and among the Dida and Avikam (Holas 1965: 76–77, 80–81).

Subsequently he began receiving frequent directives from a voice within himself that told him what to do, indicating to him how to serve God well in comforting those with problems and healing the sick. The voice told him that he could heal with the use of water that he would bless by putting his hands in it, in conjuction with the sick person's full public confession of his or her sins. The voice told him to make a cross and wrap it in white cloth. Adai's cross, like that of the Prophet Harris, became the sign of his mission (Holas 1965: 76–77, 80–81).

Boto Adai also dressed in the same style as the Prophet Harris, in a white robe with black bands crossed on the chest, and a little round white hat. On Fridays he wore a black costume of the same style to commemorate the sufferings of Christ. He always went barefoot and his followers were not allowed to wear shoes during ceremonies. Considered by his followers to be God's representative on earth, Prophet Adai's person was untouchable. He never shook anyone's hand because since it was the touch of his hands that provided the power of the curative holy water, his hands were never to be exposed to any influence that would decrease their power. He also had personal food taboos that were imposed by the angel. He did not eat red meat and ate few kinds of fish and fowl. He drank only water since alcohol was seen as a catalyzer of all kinds of sins. His followers had no food taboos, although they were to eat lightly on Friday (Holas 1965: 68-69, 77-78, 94).

The basis of Adai's teaching, drawn from his Protestant background, was the love of one God, the Ten Commandments, and the Golden Rule. Other aspects of his teaching related more directly to the traditional belief system. His followers were strictly forbidden to worship any traditional deities and to make sacrifices, as well as to possess amulets or potions to protect themselves or harm others. Witchcraft was expressly forbidden. Another important prohibition, as in the Harrist Church, was the continuation of the traditional prohibition against having sexual relations on the ground (Amos-Djoro 1956: 81, 102-103; Grivot 1942: 88).

In the public square of Adai's plantation five pedestals known as "dyiroussalem," from Jerusalem, were built in 1936. The first was composed of a small pedestal with two footprints and a large cross where public confessions were made. The second was longer, and people knelt on it, after confessing, to receive a dose of holy water. On the third, sick patients waited to be healed, and on the other two sat pails of holy water. In other villages with an Adai cult, once the location was consecrated by the local traditional chief of the land, the dyiroussalems were built. Those villages that could afford to also built a church. The church, of Protestant inspiration, was sober in style with no decor to distract members of the congregation from communicating with God. Most ceremonial activity took place around the dyiroussalems. Activity in the church occurred mainly on Sundays. There were four services preceded and succeeded by processions. The services consisted of prayers, songs, a sermon on a biblical theme, and benedictions. There were also two services on Fridays (Holas 1965: 82, 88, 97-98, 82-183).

Adai's main ritual equipment consisted of the cross and the water that had been sanctified by the touch of his hands. The Bible, particularly the aspects of the Old Testament that relate well to the local way of life, was used as inspiration for themes for sermons, but Adai did not study it, perhaps because of his insufficient education. The Bible was sometimes used to settle disputes. The two parties presented themselves before a minister and explained their cases. The minister slid a knife between two pages of the closed book and interpreted the text on the pages to which it opened in order to settle the dispute (Holas 1965: 95).

The angel who communicated with Adai said that the cross

should be wrapped in a white cloth to symbolize its purity. The cloth always had to be immaculate and was changed during a special ceremony to which only certain ministers were invited. The Prophet always had his cross with him, and when he went on an evangelizing mission it was carried in the front of his cortege by a member of his retinue. The cross was used, along with holy water, to bless plantations so that, protected from witchcraft, crops would grow well. The Prophet blessed plantations frequently in the interest of increased agricultural production (Holas 1965: 123).

The use of the holy water for drinking, washing painful parts of the body, and sometimes the asperging of plantations, was the major sacrament in the Adai cult. This water was believed to cure illnesses, neutralize the efforts of witches, make women fertile, and make plantations produce abundantly. The dosage varied little for different illnesses, and the holy water could be drunk only after a full public confession of one's sins. Some people stayed at Adai's plantation to be able to receive holy water from Adai on a daily basis for an extended period. In addition, Adai blessed certain cosmetics such as talcum powder and cologne, which could then be used prophylactically against particular occult dangers such as harm by evil spirits or witches (Amos-Djoro 1956: 296; Holas 1965: 96, 124, 131).

An individual might be ill because of being a victim of witchcraft or because of violating church rules, including that of practicing witchcraft against another person. Adai's curing method being the same for all maladies, the victim of witchcraft and the witch were treated with the same remedies. The sins confessed often involved adultery, and almost always included witchcraft, the ultimate sin (Holas 1965: 146, 148–161).

Boto Adai was the central figure in his church. Only he could heal and make holy water, and he usually officiated at sermons on his plantation. He had a corps of several ministers who assisted him on his plantation, and each village with a church had a locally selected minister. Adai and his retinue went from village to village baptizing converts and visiting active congregations. With advancing age Adai became ill and unable to travel to visit distant congregations or take care of his patients. In addition, market conditions negatively affected the financial state of his plantation community (Holas 1965: 90, 196–197).

In 1951–1952 the Adaist movement began to weaken and to be threatened by competition from other religious groups. John Ahui, extending the Harrist Church into Dida country, converted a number of Adaist villages around Divo and ordered the destruction of the dyiroussalems. In one village the inhabitants said that they had destroyed the dyiroussalems because while they believed in the Adai cult many villagers had died, a situation that they expected to remedy by following John Ahui. Ahui was assisted in spreading his church around Divo by Albert Atcho, who converted people after performing cures with herbal substances. Adai also lost members, particularly those in the interior, to another religious movement, the Deima Church. Adai died suddenly in 1963 with still a significant community of followers in the rural area south of Divo. He did not officially name a successor but it was said that he had earlier revealed the name of the person by whom he wished to be succeeded. The man in question, Paul Bédi, had a vision of Adai telling him that he had been designated, and he has become the leader of the church, but without the prestige of Boto Adai (Holas 1965: 132, 169, 203-205).

The Deima Church

There is one other movement in the Ivory Coast that grew out of the influence of the Prophet Harris. Differing from the other Ivorian movements in that it was founded by a woman and allows an important role to women, it is the Deima Church founded by Marie Lalou. Initially a dynamic and popular movement existing mainly among the Godié, Dida, Bakwé, and Bété ethnic groups, it is the second largest of the approximately 20 contemporary indigenous religious movements in the Ivory Coast, the Harrist Church being the largest. Located north of the lagoons region, the Deima Church blocked the spread to the forest area of both the Church of Boto Adai and John Ahui's Harrist Church (Barrett 1968: 20; Holas 1965: 304-305, 315).

Marie Lalou, a Godié woman, was said by some people to have been baptized by a Protestant missionary, by others to have been both Catholic and Protestant at different times, and by still others to have been neither (Holas 1965: 307; Paulme 1962: 17). Married, she had no children and one day, following instructions received in a dream, refused to continue performing her marital duties. Her husband was insistent, and he died shortly thereafter. Following custom, her late husband's brother wanted to take her as a wife. She refused, and when he died also, she was regarded with great suspicion in her husband's village (Paulme 1962: 17-18).

Returning to her own village she began to preach that God prohibited people from wishing evil to their neighbors. She distributed water that had been given her in a dream. On awakening she found it beside her bed. No one could do any harm to those who drank it with a pure heart. However, those who drank even a drop with malice in their hearts for another would ineluctably die. In the succeeding months there were many deaths in the village that were attributed to Marie Lalou whether or not the people had drunk the water. Labeled a witch, she went to another village to live with a relative but had the same problem (Paulme 1962: 17–18).

She fled to the bush and stayed there for several months until a hunter took pity on her and asked the village chief to allow her to return. He allowed her to do so. She established a church in 1942 and her fame began to spread. She began to wear a special outfit and observe numerous food taboos. Her parents wanted her to return to their village and marry. She refused, saying that God forbade her to associate with men. Her family complained to the authorities and her movement was viewed with suspicion by the colonial administration. Called to Abidjan to explain herself to the governor in 1949, she explained her doctrine. The acknowledgment of her good faith by the administration won her new converts. Shortly thereafter, following the influx of many new followers recognizing her power to heal, Marie Lalou died in 1951. She had designated a successor, Princess Jeniss, to whom she had taught the songs that had been revealed to her in dreams (Paulme 1962: 17–23).

Marie Lalou claimed to be the successor of the Prophet Harris. The Prophet Harris is mentioned in some of the written texts of the Church, and a banner for one Deima church says: "Harris Religion— Represented by Marie Lalou." The sacred texts, in which there is an occasional mention of Harris, indicate that God sent a prophet to each group of people. The texts explain the origin and nature of human society, with its differences between groups, through Bible stories that are geographically situated in Africa and adapted to fit an African milieu with local characters and characteristic events. Some combine traditional African and New Testament themes. The stated purpose of leaders of the group is to have a purely African church, led by Africans for Africans, because the Christian churches brought by the missionaries directed themselves to European concerns. The Creator God is said to have told Marie Lalou that each people had their own god (Paulme 1962: 35, 55, passim).

According to Marie Lalou the gods of the Protestants and Catholics were foreigners and therefore had no power over African witches. Since the missionaries had become influential in the African societies the evil spirits chased by the Prophet Harris had returned and were more numerous than in the past. Lalou had been chosen to chase them away and save people. She was hostile to the European missionaries at least in part because the evil spirits had returned since their arrival. The missionaries who had supposedly come to help the Africans had actually done them more harm than good. Consequently, Lalou prohibited her followers from reading or even touching the Bible, considering it to be magical. Young people were not to read it because doing so could result in mental illness (Amos-Djoro 1956: 288, 291). Lalou maintained that the rites and prayers of the missionary churches were different from those taught her in her revelations and therefore inappropriate for her people (Holas 1956: 40).

Deima religious services are celebrated twice a week, on Friday and Sunday mornings. On these days no work is done. Called to worship by a bell, the congregation meets at the home of the "prophet," as the village religious leader is called. The prophet wears a white robe on Sunday, black on Friday for the death of Christ, with a shawl over his shoulders. On his head he wears a leather miter decorated with cross insignias, and he carries a large cross. His assistants are similarly attired. The members wear their good clothes or white, and some carry small crosses. There are processions to and from the church, and the simple service consists of songs, prayers, and a short sermon. There is no communion, and only occasionally is there a public confession by a witch avowing his or her sins. The major appointments of the church consist of a tall cross wrapped in cloth, and a bottle of holy water and a container of ashes sitting on a table (Paulme 1962: 22, 75–78).

The church is structured into central and local clergies. The prophetess is assisted by a corps of 12 high-level clergymen or apostles who act as advisors. There are four other assistants: a financial officer, a housekeeper, a person to receive and show in visitors, and a representative to visit the member churches. On the local level the priests, some of whom are named by the prophetess, are assisted by advisors whom they select (Amos-Djoro 1956: 290). Some people become priests in their villages by acquiring a cross, a bell, and sacred water and ashes from the prophetess and then setting up a church (Kobben 1960: 139).

The Deima Church has a written catechism and a testament, the latter outlining the basic tenets of the religion. It is stated that the Deima religion is an ancient one originally taught by the Prophet Harris, which Marie Lalou preached as a result of her revelations. Differing from the Protestant and Catholic Churches, the Deima Church was founded to save the world from sin by making people cease worshipping their traditional deities. A village accepting the religion must begin by destroying the objects representing those deities. The church is against all evildoers and witches and everything that can do harm to people. The sacrament consists of holy water from a special source, called Deima, and ashes. While she was alive only Marie Lalou could prepare and administer the holy water. The holy water serves to heal and to protect from future harm. It protects a person from being poisoned and from falling prey to witchcraft, but one must have a pure heart when drinking it. To want to harm someone or to possess objects with which to do so is a sin in itself, so the element of moral reform is that one must struggle against all of one's own evil desires. Someone who drinks the holy water while wishing evil to another will himself or herself suffer that same evil. He or she may be cured only by confessing completely. A bottle of holy water is kept at home by members. They pray before it every morning and a few swallows are drunk on Friday morning as a protective measure. To act as a curative, the water must be administered by a member of the clergy or it can be ineffective or even harmful (Holas 1965: 314, 323; Paulme 1962: 12-14, 57, 86).

God charged Marie Lalou with the mission of destroying the traditional religious objects and of healing and eliminating witchcraft. He forbade her to use plants for healing because doing so would be similar to the technique of traditional priests and healers whom she was to combat. In addition to the holy water, however, she used ashes made from special plants that are a traditional symbol of long life because people with pure hearts will have hair as white as the ashes before they die. The ashes also provide excellent protection against witches. Sometimes the ashes are mixed with perfumed talcum powder and serve as a cosmetic that identifies members of the Deima religion (Paulme 1962: 86-88). The sacred ashes may be used, mixed with regular ones, to rub painful parts of the body (Holas 1965: 314).

After the death of Marie Lalou the Deima Church declined. Many of her followers believed that she would not die, or that she would be resurrected in 3 days. Therefore, rather than burying her immediately, they waited 5 days. Some people still believe that she will be resurrected and visit her tomb. Others among her followers left the church to join the Protestants or the Harrists, who were increasing their efforts to expand into Dida country about 1952 (Amos-Djoro 1956: 292–294). Under new leadership the movement continues to survive, though without its initial dynamism.

THE HARRIST CHURCHES COMPARED

The Prophet Harris conveyed two different messages open to ambivalent interpretations. Just as he fitted into two different roles— that of the traditional priest bringing a new and stronger indigenous deity, and that of the European missionary bringing a new religious system—Harris's behavioral message was similar to that of a traditional priest, and his verbal message to that of the missionary. The Protestants, Catholics, and Harrists emphasized different elements of his verbal message, and the Harrists attributed special significance to his behavioral message. The missionaries, particularly the Catholic missionaries, were, on the contrary, very disdainful of Harris's behavioral techniques, precisely because they were similar to those of a traditional priest. They characterized him as a charlatan and hypnotizer. They were, however, well pleased with his verbal message that merited them tens of thousands of converts.

Whereas the Harrist Church is based on a combination of both Harris's verbal and behavioral messages, the other religious movements that developed as a result of Harris's activities reflect an almost total emphasis on his behavioral message. They therefore represent a different perspective with respect to an understanding of the Prophet Harris's message. These movements took on much of the form of his activities without the essence of his intended content, thus understanding his message only partially. Taking on the form of his behavioral message, they clothed it with the traditionally oriented content that it suggested to them, rather than with the fundamental Christian content that Harris had intended. The fact that the Prophet Harris had an appeal based on his similarities to a traditional role allowed him to be understood by many people almost exclusively in the context of that role, without the realization that his contribution represented something new that was a synthesis of that role with a new one.

All of the new religious groups do share the central elements of Harris's message: to cease worshipping the traditional deities and destroy the objects representing them, as well as to respect the Sabbath and love their neighbors. However, rather than doing so in order to worship the Christian god, the members of the other religious groups have done so because the old gods are considered less effective in

healing and protecting them from witchcraft than the new one. The
Harrists, and those who became Protestant and Catholic, were also
motivated to worship the new god for pragmatic reasons. They
hoped for better health, greater prosperity, and protection from evil
and misfortune. However, these concerns are elaborated within a
larger philosophical structure, with emphasis on ethical and moral
propriety as a way to improve life in general. In the other movements, there is no such philosophical or doctrinal elaboration. Their
purpose is to heal and to eliminate the practice and effects of witchcraft, and they do so in essentially the same manner that the traditional priests and healers had used, although with some input in form
and content from the Prophet Harris. As Amos-Djoro, who considers
these movements marginal to both missionary and Harrist Christianity, said, "None of them retain anything but a veneer of Christianity
to give their ceremonies a less ancestral aspect [1956: 321–322]."

An important factor in determining the nature of the initial
message received, which was at the origin of the different kinds of
movements that developed, was geography. It has been noted that
Harris's message was propagated in different ways: by Harris himself,
by clerk-disciples designated by him, by self-designated disciples who
transmitted their versions of his message, by village delegates who
had gone to hear him and take his message back to their villages,
and by rumor. As might be expected, it was the areas that had the most
extensive and direct contact with the Prophet Harris that elaborated
his message most entirely. Harris was only in the Ivory Coast for a
short time, traveled by foot, and was not always at liberty to pursue
his mission. Consequently, his personal contacts were limited to the
coastal towns and villages. Most of his personal influence was exercised around Grand Lahou and in the Ebrié area around Abidjan and
Bingerville. He spent about 6 weeks in and around Bingerville after
returning from the Gold Coast at the time when his renown was at
its apogee. It was in these coastal areas that people joined the missionary churches and were influenced by them. However, more significantly, it was in the Grand Lahou area and in the Ebrié area that
churches that attempted to remain true to Harris by perpetuating
both his verbal and behavioral messages continued to exist.

Farther inland, the Prophet's message was carried by English-
speaking Christian clerk-disciples and by non-Christian village delegates who attempted to reconvey the Prophet's message to their fellow
villagers. It would be expected that the completeness of the convey-
ance of his message would vary with the nature of these transmitters,
and that the village delegates with no prior familiarity with Christian-

ity would transmit the most superficial version, understanding the Prophet's behavioral message much more completely than his verbal one. In the absence of further teaching, the aspects of what they understood from Harris's message that appeared most relevant to them were apparently the healing and the casting out of evil spirits, and the ritual behavior by which those ends were accomplished.

The groups that are closest to the coast are those that most fully implemented Harris's message. It is in the coastal area that the missionary influence was strongest and where the populations became most christianized. The Ebrié, who form the majority of the Harrist Church, are 99% Christian, as are the Alladian, who also constitute a large proportion of church membership. And it is on the coast that the Harrist Church has had its greatest success. The farther one goes inland, the more the Christian religious influence decreases and the percentage of partisans of the traditional religions increases.

This tendency is reflected in the geographical distribution of the Harrist churches of different orientations. None of the new religious movements has significant memberships in Abidjan, the capital. The Harrist Church is essentially peri-urban, having the majority of its churches located in the villages around Abidjan, although a very few are in Ebrié village areas that have been incorporated into the city. The movements oriented exclusively toward healing and the elimination of witchcraft are located in the interior, mainly in rural villages around inland towns. Thus, with increased distance from urban areas, the content of the movement reflects a less Christian and more traditional orientation.

As one would expect from the geographical locations and religious orientations of the various movements, the Harrist Church is more progressively oriented than the others in both an ideological and a practical sense. More of its members participate in the modern sector of the economy and more have acquired the requisite literacy and skills with which to do so than is the case for members of the groups located in the rural interior. Harrist Church leaders are concerned with the nature of the church's relationship to the modern sector and wish it to play an important role in it. Such is far less the case for the rural groups that have little real contact with this modern sector and whose concerns remain quite traditionally oriented.

In addition to the differences between the cues given by Harris's behavioral and verbal messages, another important factor in determining what the groups he inspired did was what he did not say, those aspects of life about which he made no comment but with which the new religions had to deal. In some areas he gave directives that he failed to give in others, and he apparently made no comments at all about some issues that the new movements had to face. The directives of the disciples were of necessity less complete than those of the Prophet, and, except for the basic elements of the message, undoubtedly differed some according to the disciples' own orientations. This contribution by the disciples was a factor in lending variation to the developing movements. Those village delegates who returned home to share Harris's teachings with their neighbors had the least complete knowledge of Harris's teachings on the basis of which to pursue their new religious course.

In all of the movements when situations or questions arose for which there were no specific directives from the Prophet, the leaders decided what to institutionalize as the proper course of behavior. These decisions were usually attributed to Harris post hoc. Sometimes the course of action chosen was to perpetuate traditional forms. In other cases one of the missionary churches furnished the model, and in many cases ad hoc decisions became institutionalized as policy.

For example, in the Harrist Church there is no sacrament for marriage. The Prophet Harris did not say there should be one, consequently for the Harrists marriages have continued to be celebrated according to the traditional pattern. Borrowing from the Catholic Church appears in the costumes of the prophets of the Deima Church, although Harris provided an adequate sartorial model. Deima prophets wear long robes with stoles and miters. In the case of the organization of the Crastchotche, the church structure includes four ministers because one of Makoui's successors originally selected four ministers to direct the church.

The most significant aspect of Harris's activity, which served as the basis for the formation of all of the subsequent movements, was his discrediting of the traditional deities. He demonstrated concretely that the god he represented was stronger and more effective in healing and protecting than the old gods, and indicated that by following his techniques others could assure themselves of the new god's help and protection. In addition, after having accepted Harris's baptism, his converts could no longer return to their former religious practices. In so doing, Harris inadvertently paved the way for the subsequent movements that developed by creating a situation in which new religious orientations had to be developed and by saying that teachers would come along to continue his work. He said that his mission was to baptize, thus to prepare the way for others. Those teachers, inspired by Harris's example, could legitimate themselves and their program by claiming to be his successors, from the European Protestant missionaries to Marie Lalou.

The Prophet Harris provided a new spiritual charter by which others, saying they came in his name, could establish themselves. He came into a sociocultural system ordered and maintained by spiritual sanctions with a new mandate from a more powerful spiritual source. The religious leaders who succeeded him thus obtained their authority by claiming a link with the Prophet Harris to associate themselves with this new spiritual mandate. By creating a situation in which people could acquire authority by saying that they came in his name, Harris opened the way for the development of a host of diverse religious possibilities. By paving a way to religious change from which there was no turning back, he created a situation in which new religious phenomena were an inevitable outcome. His activities destroyed the old religious structure and created the necessity for and the possibility of the development of new structures, albeit based on reinterpretations of old behaviors. He provided the impetus for the three different forms of restructuring—that of the missionaries, that of the Harrists, and that of the healing and anti-witchcraft cults.

A comparison of the religious movements that developed out of Harris's influence will indicate the nature of the leader's perception of his or her relationship to Harris and the aspects of the Prophet's message that each chose to elaborate, as well as the kinds of directions in which the movements developed. Jonas Zaka, who became a Methodist minister, did not claim to be a successor of Harris's or to have had a divine revelation telling him to start a new movement. He had been true to Harris by joining the Methodist Church. However, the fact that he decided that it was possible to be Christain without being dominated by Europeans who demanded changes in the African social life was probably spurred by the example of the Prophet Harris, the first person from whom he learned about Christianity, and whose Christianity, as the Ivorians perceived it, was independent of the Europeans and accepting of and congruent with the African life-style.

Boto Adai apparently saw himself as called to the same kind of mission as was the Prophet Harris because he said that he did not feel that he could be as strong as Harris in overcoming adversity. Bodjo Aké claimed to have taken the place of both Harris and God, whereas Makoui diminished Harris's role to merely foretelling his own coming. This latter Harris had indeed done when he said that people would come to continue his teaching. Ironically, Makoui's church, however, rather than showing much originality as a result of its founder's input, is of all the movements the one that is the most similar to John Ahui's Harrist Church, which tried to be the most faithful to Harris. The name Crastchotche, comes from Harris (some Harrist churches have written on their facades in English, "Christ Church"), and the bell ringers and guardians, plus the schedule of services, appear to be patterned directly on those of the Harrists. Perhaps this is the result of Makoui's followers' stay in the Ebrié village. Like the Harrists, their main collective prayer is also the Lord's prayer.

Marie Lalou claimed to preach the religion founded by Harris, but as the Deima Church has evolved, there has been increasingly less mention of Harris as Lalou's predecessor, and much mythology has grown up around Lalou as the founder of the church, and around her successors. Gaston N'Drin perpetuated in Grand Lahou the tradition of the churches that Harris had told people to build to worship independently, and John Ahui, Harris's most direct successor, claimed no special revelation but saw his task as that of expanding and consolidating Harris's work. Harris is seen by the Harrists as in the same position as Jesus Christ, but as God's prophet to the Africans. The Deimaists also believed that God sent each people a prophet and that Marie Lalou was theirs.

Grace Thannie, who had accompanied Harris, undertook to continue his work, but the church she founded, although claiming Harris as the authority for everything it does, has diverged almost completely from his teachings and has evolved many original forms uninspired by the Prophet. It is isolated from the Harris-inspired churches of the Ivory Coast. Therefore, rather than being influenced by them, it is influenced by the spiritualist churches of Ghana, with which it is associated, and it has more in common with them than with the Ivorian groups. As for Bébéh Gra's and Papa Nouveau's claims not to have been inspired by Harris, both claims are implausible given the tremendous influence Harris exercised in the areas in which both developed their movements and had their greatest success. Harris's fame did not really grow until after he had passed through Sassandra, from which Bébéh Gra came, and Papa Nouveau had much of his influence in the Grand Lahou area in which Harris had caused the original religious ferment. Papa Nouveau's influence and his church show marked similarities to the avowedly Harris-inspired groups. It is thus more reasonable to interpret Papa Nouveau's claim that he is not a successor to the Prophet Harris as an attempt to establish himself as his own authority source. Also, his legitimacy in people's eyes comes from his association with an important traditional cult rather than with Harris.

Another feature on which the different movements vary is their attitudes toward the missionaries and the missionary churches. Since the Bible was associated with the missionary churches, particularly with the Protestant church, the attitude toward the Bible is related to the attitude toward the missionaries. The concern of most of these movements is more with the Protestant than with the Catholic missionaries because it was the former who made the most energetic attempts to win over Harris' converts, and so were competitors for members with these movements.

Both Zaka and N'Drin had good rapport with the Protestants, although both wished to worship independently of them. Zaka separated from the missionaries for more social autonomy, and N'Drin's church developed autonomously and remained so, although getting assistance from the Protestants. Both emphasized reading the Bible. Adai saw no conflict between setting up his own church when called by God to do so, and being a good Methodist, and he used biblical texts as inspiration for his sermons.

Ahui and Aké developed their movements in opposition to the Protestant missionaries, whom both saw as intending to exploit the Africans financially. Their opposition to the missionaries was also a result of the disruption the latter were causing in their respective societies by diminishing the power of the old men and creating greater influence for the young men. Aké was overtly against the Bible because young men taught to read it had a new source of knowledge with which to challenge the elders. This was also a concern of Ahui's and an issue in his conflict with N'Drin about who was most true to Harris. Ahui's church had lost many of its young people to the Protestant church that provided them with the modern skill of literacy. However, Ahui's Harrists felt that it was always necessary to have a Bible in church, even if it was not read, because it contained the Word of God, and now that there are literate members, it is read.

Marie Lalou felt that the Protestant missionaries had done more harm than the good they had supposedly come to do for the Africans in that since their arrival, the evil spirits chased by the Prophet Harris had returned. Consequently, she forbade her followers, especially young people for whom it was particularly dangerous, to read the Bible. The Deima cult developed its own written texts that did include biblical stories and themes. They were, however, modified to fit both their African milieu and Marie Lalou's purposes.

Harrists feel that they are better Christians than the members of the Protestant and Catholic churches because, whereas their church absolutely forbids reliance on any spiritual support other than God, the missionary churches do not have the kinds of sanctions the Harrists have against doing so. People who violated Harris's injunctions in this area when he was in the Ivory Coast supposedly died. Therefore some Harrists suspect that Protestants and Catholics sometimes seek the kind of spiritual support that their churches do not provide from indigenous sources, and, although supposedly Christian, may "have something in their pockets." Harrists also feel that the Protestant and Catholic churches cannot deal with specifically African sins, such as having sexual relations on the ground, and especially witchcraft. Such is also the attitude of the Deimaists. Marie Lalou claimed that the foreign missionary churches could not fight against evil spirits as her specifically African church did, but, on the contrary, contributed to their proliferation. The Church of the Twelve Apostles considered affiliating with a missionary church until they decided that the latter wanted to take away their power to fight evil spirits by prohibiting the use of the gourd rattles. Rejection of these particular missionaries did not indicate a general hostility to the missionary churches, although church members do feel that the Protestants do not have the faith necessary for healing, and church leaders cite the Bible to justify some of their practices.

In other cases also elements of the Bible have been used to give increased meaning to behavior irrespective of the attitude toward the missionaries. Examples are the Jerusalems (hozalem, dyiroussalem) of Boto Adai, Soboa Obodji, and Papa Nouveau, and the wearing of different colored costumes on different days of the week by Adai, in the Crastchotche, and by the Deima prophets in response to biblical events. Actually, as the movements evolve, adapt to contemporary conditions, and have a larger number of literate members, the Bible acquires greater significance in spite of earlier attitudes toward it. It increasingly replaces as the basis of authority both the Prophet Harris and the particular founder of the movement. With greater literacy also comes the tendency to compile written texts in an attempt to elaborate and standardize the doctrine and to make it available for accurate transmission. This trend exists among the Twelve Apostles, the Harrists, the Adaists, and the Deimaists.

Consequently, the attitudes of the various groups toward the missionaries and the missionary churches vary: from the belief that the missionaries are fulfilling Harris's prediction by teaching the Africans; to an appreciation of the missionaries in spite of the desire to have an autonomous structure; to a positive feeling toward them although there is no real contact between the particular movement and the missionary churches; to opposition to them for disrupting the indigenous social order, for allegedly wanting to exploit the Africans financially, and for being ineffective or detrimental in the fight against the most significant form of evil, witchcraft.

There are important differences between the organizational structures of the different groups. The only organizational directive given by Harris was that a minister and 12 apostles should be selected to direct the religious life of each village. The Church of Twelve Apostles is so called for this reason, but has no apostles in evidence. The Harrist Church and Crastchotche have apostles who are the church administrators, and Marie Lalou's advisors were called apostles. Aside from this suggestion from the Prophet, the movements' organizational structures were developed by their leaders. The structural feature most determining of the dynamics of the movement has been the nature of the leadership and the degree of centralization of authority. The churches of Boto Adai and Marie Lalou contrast with the Church of the Twelve Apostles, and the Harrist Church falls between. Both Adai and Marie Lalou received revelations empowering them to heal. Theirs was not a power that either could delegate to others, so, although churches loyal to them could be set up in scattered villages with local ministers, only the founders could bless the sacramental water and heal, and therefore they remained the physical, geographical, and spiritual centers of the highly centralized structures. Since the leaders' powers could not be delegated, there was a limit to the possible geographical spread of the movements, although both leaders had successors.

The Church of the Twelve Apostles has a regional administrative structure but no single leader. Local ministers are autonomous, and a person may become a prophet with all privileges by finding out if he or she has the necessary gifts of healing and prophecy, and then going through a period of training with an established prophet or prophetess. Any gifted person who successfully acquires the necessary knowledge and techniques may set up a garden and receive patients, so authority within the structure is thoroughly decentralized and accessible to many, which makes expansion a simple matter.

In the Harrist Church the only divine revelation was that of the Prophet Harris, who designated John Ahui as a continuer of his work. Ahui, a "secular organizer," designated others to assist him in the task of spreading Harris's teachings. Village ministers are selected by the village and approved by Ahui, and villages that would like to establish a Harrist Church may select a minister and send him to Ahui for approval and instruction. Thus there is a centralized structure but authority can be delegated, and the qualities necessary to be able to receive such a delegation of authority may be learned, rather than being dependent upon innate gifts or spiritual revelations.

On the ritual level there are great similarities in the key features of most of the churches. Most visibly striking is the fact that Boto Adai, the prophets in the Church of the Twelve Apostles, and John Ahui and the ministers of the Harrist Church all dressed or dress like the Prophet Harris. Baptism is the key rite in all of the churches and indicates that the individual renounces all practices associated with the traditional deities. A version of Harris's baptism, which was similar to traditional rites of washing to purify from sin and protect from evil, has become institutionalized as the essential sacrament in the healing cults. Water is blessed and then used for drinking as a medicine or for washing as a curative and protective agent. The Prophet Harris blessed the water by touching it with his cross, and the Twelve Apostles hold it up to the cross and pray over it. Among the Harrists its power came from the minister's prayers, whereas Adai could make it holy with his touch, and Lalou got it from a special source and prayed over it.

The cross is essential to all of the groups as a repository of great power that can protect from evil, and as a symbol of its spiritual mission, which is to convert people away from their indigenous religions. Harris's cross was believed to be the home of a strong spirit, and the crosses found in the various churches and carried by the ministers are thought to share the same quality. Ceremonies having to do with the cross, such as the installation of one in church, may be attended only by spiritually pure and powerful people and must be performed in secret.

The four elements of the Prophet Harris's ritual accoutrements were the Bible, the gourd bowl of baptismal water, the cross, and the gourd rattle. The rattles, which are used in the Harrist Church, Crastchotche, and the Church of the Twelve Apostles, continue to have their traditional dual function of being musical instruments and of chasing away or overcoming evil spirits and transmitting people's prayers to God. This is so in spite of the fact that nothing indicates that Harris used the rattles other than as musical instruments, just as his efforts to convince people that his cross did not contain a strong spirit were also unsuccessful.

The Prophet Harris insisted on certain standards for social behavior, such as prohibiting adultery, alcoholism, theft and lying. These prohibitions, although already institutionalized in the indigenous societies, along with respect for the Sabbath, were made part of their doctrine by all of the groups, each with its own nuances about alcohol, smoking, and food taboos. Violation of these and other church rules, for both the Adaists and the Harrists, involves punishment in the form of carrying heavy bricks around the church in public view. Harris urged changes in some customs, such as having long expensive funerals and the practice of asking the cadaver who was responsible for his or her death. These and other social modifications have been made by the various groups. Harris said that he tolerated polygamy but preferred monogamy. The fact that he was accompanied by two, and sometimes three women, apparently suggested to his audiences that he was a partisan of polygamy, which all of the groups permit. Even Zaka, in spite of being Methodist, allowed polygamy, one of the indigenous social institutions that he felt the missionaries attacked unjustly.

Another prohibition that exists explicitly in all of the groups forbids having sexual relations on the ground. A major part of the doctrine of certain groups, specifically attributed to Harris by some, it is really an important traditional prohibition that has been incorporated by the new religious institutions and given new sanctions, indicating that it is still a very important area of concern.

A most significant moral departure from the traditional world view in the movements inspired by Harris has occurred in the locus of responsibility for good and evil. The major source of evil in the indigenous societies was and is witchcraft, in which one person wishes another evil, and the proposed victim subsequently suffers misfortune, be it physical illness or a particularly scanty harvest or fishing catch. In the traditional belief system it was believed that a person who was wealthy and powerful must have acquired such a status by using witchcraft to harm his neighbors in order to acquire more than his share of wealth and also to protect himself from being harmed by jealous people. Thus the practice of witchcraft was thought to accrue positive benefits to the perpetrator.

In the Harris-inspired movements the perpetrator does not benefit from harming others, but is himself punished. The Christian message of just desserts for those who seek to harm others was integrated as a replacement for the prevailing principle. In the new movements the person who seeks to harm another is sinning against God by violating the Golden Rule. Most of the new religious groups, in addition to stating that one should love one's neighbors, also emphasize in one or several commandments beyond the standard ten that one must not harm one's neighbors, either directly or through witchcraft. Some groups say only that one must not "eat human flesh and drink human blood," the general metaphor for witchcraft, whereas others enumerate more specifically that one should not change oneself into an animal to eat a neighbor's crops and spoil his plantation, or "attach" or "sell" a woman's womb to make her sterile, etc.

According to the new morality, in some groups the witches fall sick for their misdeeds, and in others it is expected that they themselves will suffer the same misfortune desired for their intended victims. When people seek to be healed, sometimes they feel that they are, and they are judged by the healer to be, the victims of witchcraft. More often, however, they confess to having sought to harm others—to having themselves committed the sin of performing witchcraft.

The significance of this very important change lies in the locus of responsibility for evil in the world and in the consequences of perpetrating such evil. Witchcraft is a major perennial social problem in the societies in question because it is the explanatory mechansim for all otherwise unexplainable misfortune. Consequently, it constitutes the greatest crime against the society. In the past those people who perpetrated the most misfortune on other members of the community were actually rewarded for their misdeeds because it was they who reaped the society's benefits in the form of wealth, power, and prestige. Those who did not do evil did not benefit because they were good but, on the contrary, often suffered at the hands of witches. Thus, the change in the ethical doctrine has been that those who attempt to do evil to others, rather than achieving greater personal success for their efforts, are themselves punished, not by the community but by God. Only by avowing their crimes may their punishment be terminated. Those people who do not try to harm others should not themselves have to fear being harmed. Consequently, those individuals who create evil in the world are their own victims because the evil should turn back on them before reaching its intended victims. As a sign on the front of one Harrist Church says: "If you do good, it is for you. If you do evil, it is for you."

Each individual should now be solely responsible for his or her own fate, and rather than trying to succeed by harming others, each person should work hard for his or her own success, which should be forthcoming. Such an ideal situation has not yet entirely come into existence, of course, or these religious movements, like most others in the world, would have no raison d'être. Therefore, they exist to heal those who have been victims of witchcraft, since some people still manage to get away with it, but even more to help those people who cause the misfortune in society to change their ways so that evil and misfortune will cease to exist. Members of each of the different movements stress the fact that life has gotten so much better and people are so much less evil than they were prior to the founding of their own religious group.

It is significant that Harris's teachings did not suggest that his intent was to lead to the creation of anti-witchcraft healing cults. His success and the fact that his influence was able to lead so many people to pursue what they understood to be his intent in so many different directions suggests that his message had much broader implications. In reality, accounts of his teaching dating from the period, as well as accounts of what Harris did and said gathered recently from old men in the Harrist Church, do not indicate that Harris specifically addressed himself to the problem of evil in the form of witchcraft, just as there is no indication that healing was one of his major activities. Harris probably did touch on and give advice on witchcraft and healing, just as he gave advice on funerals. Neither, however, was the focus of his activities nor had the importance attributed to them by most of the movements founded in his name.

Harris's stated purpose, which his activities suggest was indeed his actual intent, was to change the basis of the religious orientation of his audiences. He offered them salvation through the worship of a deity very reminiscent of their own High God in replacement for the lesser deities whom they had been worshipping. This more powerful god would provide them with far greater help and protection which would lead to an improvement in the general quality of life and to greater prosperity. Harris's emphasis was on converting people to the worship of his god and on changing aspects of their social behavior that were in conflict with his essentially Protestant background. The problem of evil was therefore only one facet of his concern. His major intent was apparently to inspire broad spiritual and consequently behavioral changes. He brought new knowledge and new goals and taught the ways of attaining them. The major goal was to learn to worship the Christian god correctly, which would lead to a better and more prosperous life free from misfortune. The way of attaining these goals was to stop all worship of the traditional deities, go to church or build one in which to pray to God, and learn to read the Bible to know God's will and to learn to behave in accordance with it. Essentially a Christian missionary, his intent was to Christianize—to provide a new theology, a new world view with changed moral and ethical components, and a new formal religious structure that would allow people to develop and actualize new concepts of their own possibilities. His teachings were broadly based, touching on many aspects of social relations internal to the societies in question as well as in their relationship to the developing larger society. The most complete implementations of his teachings in the Harrist Church resulted in the creation of a dynamic institution oriented toward adapting to the changing demands of the modernizing national society. The church is increasingly developing in the direction that Harris seems to have intended.

The movements derived from Harris's influence, mediated through the various founders discussed, in no way involve such a broad application of Harris's teachings. They lack the broad concerns and are more traditionally oriented. Their geographical location reinforces this orientation, not making great demands on them to change their life style. Their major concern is with the perennial problem of witchcraft, and the new religious structures provide ways of dealing with it that are actually variations on the old theme. Whereas the Harrist Church developed to a large extent as an attempt to create a new institution predicated on Harris's teachings, the groups founded by the later prophets rather adapted selected aspects of Harris's teachings for implementation in accordance with their own concerns.

Harris's entire message, where implemented, provided the basis for the establishment of a dynamic institution, and it is the degree of implementation of Harris's message, broad concerns, and more progressive orientation that distinguishes the Harrist Church from the other movements. Its strategic location, its organizational structure, and its broadly based concerns, as well as its progressive orientation augur well for it in comparison with the other groups, from which it has gathered members as they have declined. Barrett indicates that African movements without a Christian base that are mainly concerned with witchcraft eradication are usually short lived because people become disillusioned. Religious movements last only if they provide solutions relevant to long-term trends in the society, and thus are assured a continued source of new recruits (Barrett 1968: 238). People are likely to become disillusioned with movements dedicated solely to healing and eliminating witchcraft because the healing sometimes fails and the evils of witchcraft still exist. Thus, the new religion has little further to offer them. In addition, these movements are not progressively oriented and do little to help their members adapt successfully to the changing larger society. The Harrist Church, on the contrary, has been progressively evolving into a more modern institution exercising an increasingly greater role in more and more facets of its members' lives. It subsumes the anti-witchcraft healing function in parts of its doctrine, and intensively in its practice through the work of Albert Atcho, while the main body of the church structure concerns itself with more general aspects of life.

REFERENCES

Amos-Djoro, E. 1956 *Prophetisme et Nationalisme Africains: Les Harristes en Côte d'Ivoire.* Paris: Ecole Pratique des Hautes Etudes, Section des Religions, Manuscrit.

Augé, M. 1969 *Le Rivage Alladian: Organisation et Evolution des Villages Alladian.* Paris: Orstom.

Baeta, C. G. 1962 *Prophetism in Ghana.* London: S.C.M. Press, Ltd.

Barrett, D. F. 1968 *Schism and Renewal in Africa: An Analysis of Six Thousand Contemporary Religious Movements.* Nairobi: Oxford University Press.

Bernus, E. 1957 "Ahouati: Notes sur un Village Dida," *Etudes Eburnéenes,* 6, 213–229.

Bonnefoy, C. 1954 "Tiagba: Notes sur un Village Aizi," *Etudes Eburnéenes,* 3, 7–129.

Bureau, R. 1971 *Le Prophète Harris et la Religion Harriste (Côte d'Ivoire).* Ivory Coast: Université d'Abidjan, Institut d' Ethnosociologie.

Grivot, R. 1942 "Le Cercle de Lahou (Côte d'Ivoire)." *Bulletin de L'Institut Français d'Afrique Noire,* 4, 1–4, 1–154.

Haliburton, G. M. 1971 *The Prophet Harris.* London: Longmans Group, Ltd.

Holas, B. 1965 *Le Séparatisme Religieux en Afrique Noire.* Paris: Presses Universitaires de France.

Köbben, A. J. F. 1960 "Prophetic Movements as an Expression of Social Protest," *International Archives of Ethnography,* 59, Part 1.

Paulme, D. 1962 "Une Religion Syncrétique en Côte d'Ivoire: le Culte Deima," *Cahiers d'Etudes Africaines,* 3, 9, 1ᵉcah, 5–90.

Walker, S. 1976 *Christianity African Style: The Harrist Church of the Ivory Coast.* Unpublished Ph.D. dissertation, University of Chicago.

Weber, M. 1947 *The Theory of Social and Economic Organization,* translated by A. M. Henderson and Talcott Parsons, Talcott Parsons (ed.). New York: Oxford University Press.

Worsley, P. 1968 *The Trumpet Shall Sound.* New York: Schocken Books.

Yando, E. 1970 *L'Evolution du Harrisme en Côte d'Ivoire.* Thèse préparée pour une License en Théologie, Faculté de Théologie Protestante de Paris.

II
Leith Mullings

RELIGIOUS CHANGE AND SOCIAL STRATIFICATION IN LABADI, GHANA
The Church of The Messiah

I

African Christian churches have emerged in the context of rapidly changing social relationships. The study of African Christian movements has underscored the problem of elaborating a theory of religion which can take cognizance of the process of social change. Many scholars view the rise of these churches as a response to changes in social organization. Although there is little agreement about specific antecedent factors relevant to large-scale conversion to Christianity, they have tended to focus on changes in the "scale" of society. Wilson (1969:25), for example, argues that the most general characteristic of rapid social change in Africa relevant to changing religious systems is "change in scale," involving the number of people interacting; Peel (1968:8) suggests that the rise of towns and their characteristic features, such as literacy and "an absence of ties with paganism" may be necessary structural prerequisites for the development of African Christian churches;[1] Horton (1971: 102) suggests

1. However, he does not consider these factors sufficient explanation for the content of religious behavior, seeking the "essence" of religion in its "rational" function.

65

AFRICAN CHRISTIANITY
Patterns of Religious Continuity

that the decisive factor in religious change in West African societies has been the change from the "microcosm" of the local community to the "macrocosm" of the wider world. Whereas demographic transformations, the development of communications, and new economic and political boundaries are clearly preconditions for large-scale conversion, my research among spiritualist churches in southeastern Ghana, indicated that there is a need to look more specifically at the significance of the new forms of stratification that are basic to the emerging social relationships. This chapter, then, is concerned with exploring some of the relationships between the ideology and ritual of an African Christian church in southeastern Ghana and these new forms of social stratification.

Christianity was introduced into Ghana in the seventeenth century. The emergence of African Christian churches, given impetus by the visit of the Grebo prophet, Harris, to Ghana (then the Gold Coast) in 1913, occurred in the context of the European colonial thrust and the nationalist reaction against it. Not surprisingly, the nature of the relationship between colonialism, nationalism, and African churches has been subject to disagreement.[2] By 1970, there were approximately 300 African Christian churches in Ghana (Opoku 1970); some were a result of schism from a mother church and others were founded by an individual. These churches are usually referred to as "spiritualist" churches (sometimes termed "spiritist" or "spiritual") because of their invocation of the "holy spirit." This category includes a wide variety of churches: those that are, at some level, associated with international African movements (e.g., Harrists or Aladura), as well as hundreds of single churches, associated with particular individuals and known only within local areas.

I propose to examine the Church of the Messiah, one of the local, spiritualist churches in Labadi, a town in southeastern Ghana, focusing on some of the relationships between ritual and belief and the emerging pattern of social relationships based on new forms of hierarchy, and a qualitatively different relationship between the individual and the collectivity. To this end I will (*a*) describe the major

---

2. Baeta (1962:4), for example, does not consider the main thrust of the African Christian church movement in Ghana to be a reflection of nationalist tendencies. He does, however, document a clash between an African Christian church group under Prophet Appiah and the colonial police, following Appiah's declaration of his intention to march to Accra to free the prisoners held in Ussler Fort Prison. Opoku (1970:8) on the other hand, suggests that the development of independent churches is a component of the general thrust toward "African self-expression."

changes in social organization that have taken place in this area of Ghana, (*b*) outline some of the rituals and ideologies of this spiritualist church with emphasis on how they differ from traditional religion, and (*c*) discuss the relationships between social stratification and religious developments.

II

Labadi is a coastal Ga town of approximately 26,000 within the city limits of Accra, the capital of Ghana. Before extensive European intrusion, it was a settlement of farmers and fishermen in which rights to the major means of production, land, were essentially equal. Most aspects of social life, including access to land, were organized through the lineage structure. The political organization of the town was based upon complementary relationships among lineage groups, through which individuals had rights to statuses and offices.

Although Ga society was constantly being modified by its relationship with other African groups,[3] the arrival of Europeans during the sixteenth century and the changes they brought about through slave "trade" and colonialism laid the basis for qualitative alterations in social and economic relations. An increasing volume of trade with the Europeans drew the coastal people into a wider framework of relationships. During the initial period of mercantile trade, Europeans (individual and state-chartered firms) seldom ventured inland. Much of the trade remained in the hands of Africans, particularly Fanti and Ga, resulting in the development of a new stratum of African middlemen who acted as liaisons between African and European traders. The European presence on the coast also resulted in an increased demand for African skilled and unskilled labor. A major modification produced by the mercantile period, then, was the emergence of a small stratum of Ga merchants and wage-workers. The Basel Mission played a significant role in this process by opening a workshop in 1857 at Christianborg—the town contiguous to Labadi. In addition to being a major employer of labor, the Basel mission also trained skilled laborers (to be used by the Europeans) such as blacksmiths, mechanics, and shoemakers (Szereszewski, 1975:8, Kimble, 1963:7).

3. Contact with other African groups through migration, trade, and warfare, as well as modification in the productive forces seems to have resulted in the precipitation of smaller units of production and consumption on one hand and the creation of larger territorial units, such as federations and towns, on the other.

The conditions of colonialism—including the imposition of a money economy and the development of a labor force through commoditization of the land,[4] taxation and forced labor—further hastened the dissolution of the traditional social–economic system of the village community.[5] The sale of land was instrumental in transforming the egalitarian relations of production into unequal ones. A small group of individuals benefited, while others were pushed into the work force. With the decline of equal access to collectively owned land,[6] and the emergence of new forms of wealth based on an increasingly complex division of labor, class stratification, as defined by differing access to the means of production, developed. This horizontal differentiation of the lineage appears to have occurred in the relatively recent past. The 1891 census reports that the primary occupations of Labadians were farming and fishing,[7] with some petty trading "on the increase." By the 1960 census approximately 72% of the population was reported to be employed in mining and quarrying, manufacturing, construction, commerce, transport, storage, and communication, as opposed to 8% employed in agriculture (some of whom continue to farm collectively owned land). Labadi is characterized by a proliferation of small enterprises: the majority of women, 73.8%, are listed as working in "commerce" (mainly petty trading), and the majority of the 12.7% of employed males and 9.8% of employed females listed as working in manufacturing, are self-employed.[8]

The category of "services," in which 23% of employed males and 11.8% of employed females are said to work is highly heterogeneous: it includes clerical workers, managers, civil servants, bureaucrats, and intellectual elements. The replacement of expatriates with local cadre and the expansion of the state bureaucracy makes this stratum a rapidly growing sector of the occupational structure in many postcolonial societies. Often upper levels of this stratum have the potential to develop an elite life-style through: (1) the relatively high income due to the shortage of trained personnel and the fact

4. By this term I refer to the fact that land could be bought and sold.

5. By "village community," I refer to the form of social organization, at one time widespread in West Africa, that is based on agricultural production by small farmers, where technology is relatively simple and the major means of production, land, is collectively owned.

6. By 1972, approximately 3/5 of Labadi land was privately owned or owned by the national government.

7. Fishing appears to have become differentiated more rapidly than farming.

8. Unemployment was reported to be 11%.

that the salary scale is often adjusted to the expatriate level and (2) the potential of this stratum for direct participation in local and national politics. Thus there is a high level of aspiration to this stratum. Reporting on investigations in Ghana, Jahoda (1966:199-200) noted that approximately two-thirds to three-quarters of his sample of parents questioned about their hopes for their children, and the same proportion of the sample, of young people themselves, aspired to professional, or at least white collar, jobs. Because Western education is a prerequisite for entry into this stratum, education is universally perceived as necessary for acquiring an "elite," or even a comfortable, life-style.[9] As we shall note, there is an intimate connection between Western education and Christianity, with respect to both the institutional connection between Christian churches and schools and the underlying transformation in orientation and values that is related to the conversion from traditional religion to Christianity.

In Labadi, then, social change has been characterized by growing social stratification. With the development of wage labor and widespread private property in the form of privately owned land, houses, or businesses, the significance of the lineage as a relatively homogeneous wealth-holding unit is altered as farmers become wage or salary workers, petty traders, or small or medium-sized businessmen. Collectively held wealth and cooperative labor are replaced with individual enterprise, individual wages, salaries, and private property. An integral aspect of this process, then, is increasing individualization, the process by which the individual assumes, at the expense of the kinship group, a greater responsibility for his own welfare.[10] The process of individualization was evident in all areas of life in Labadi. Individuals (or nuclear families) assumed more responsibility for the lineage, not only for subsistence and livelihood, but also for debts, education, care of children, choice of marriage partners,

9. Jahoda (1966:204) has noted that education is seen as "the key to status and affluence." Owusu (1970:92) describes the relationship between education, wealth, and power in Ghana as follows: "Superior education itself leads to wealth and wealth is a means to the organization of power, which in turn may lead to more wealth and to higher social status and prestige."

10. This process is similar to that described by Mintz (1974:310) among the rural proletarians involved in the transition from family-owned *hacienda* relationships to those of U. S.-based corporate planation enterprises in Puerto Rico:

> By "individualization" is meant here that the objectification of labor and the alienation of the laborer enable the individual to objectify himself, particularly as regards the traditional social forms which, until the advent of modern factory-style capitalism, interfered with precisely this kind of self-objectification.

and rites of passage (Mullings 1975, Chapter 1). Labadians of all social strata themselves perceived this process and invariably refer to the emergence of individual interests in describing changing patterns of life. This widely held view was most graphically expressed by a farmer who, in concluding his discussion of the replacement of co-operative labor with individual labor stated, "Today everyone paddles his own canoe." I will suggest that the deemphasis of the kinship group and emphasis on the individual is one of the major themes reflected in the spiritualist churches.

III

Before discussing the spiritualist churches, I will outline some of the relevant features of the indigenous religions. Traditional religion, which includes autochthonous deities as well as those introduced by the interaction between African groups, continues to be widely practiced among townspeople. The basis of public worship is the seven town-lineage gods; each of the seven maximal lineages has charge of one of these gods and is represented in public worship by an elder of that lineage who serves as his priest. Through control of supernatural power, elders are able to exert a certain degree of influence. However, highly structured traditions governing the behavior of these representatives limits the extent to which such a position can be used for individual ends. The goal of public worship is to ensure blessings for the entire community as represented by the seven maximal lineages; the major concerns are bounty, fertility, and victory in war. The dynamics of public worship are most graphically expressed in the annual central ritual that is performed over a period of 6 months. The ritual units involved are the seven maximal lineages, as represented by the priests of the town-lineage gods. The lineages are represented as corporate groups; the individual, as such, is not recognized in public worship. None of the ritual episodes can be celebrated properly without the attendance of all representatives of the lineages, emphasizing the equality and complementarity among lineages. Each phase of ritual activity is structured, with particular roles assigned to the representative priests and spirit mediums. Through various ritualized activities, including agricultural activities, gift exchange, invocation, sacrifice, drumming, singing, and possession, and through the use of such symbols as water and colors, the values of traditional society are projected, with particular emphasis on egalitarianism, complementarity, and kinship obligations.[11]

Traditional healing reinforces the precepts of the village community and traditional religion. Illness and healing are considered to be the responsibility of the lineage as a whole, and members of the lineage and family have structured roles in the major curing rituals. Failure to participate in the treatment process may incur suspicion of responsibility for the illness of the patient. In the vast majority of the cases that I witnessed, the healer identified the source of the illness as ultimately resulting from some disturbance of relationships within the lineage or extended family. Treatment, then, involves the restructuring of these relationships, *on the basis of* the traditional norms of the village community. For example, in one fairly typical case of a market woman, her illness was attributed to her mother's sister's daughter's jealousy at her successful accumulation of capital from marketing. At the treatment ritual, where attendance of kin was mandatory, her kin were admonished to remember that her money was their money (although this was, in fact, no longer the case since private ownership of profits from marketing was by this time generally accepted.)

While traditional religion developed in the context of lineage-based village community, Christianity emerged as this type of society was giving way to new structure. Although there are 3 "orthodox" Christian churches in Labadi—Presbyterian, Anglican, and Catholic—mass participation in Christianity is dominated by the spiritualist churches. In 1970-1972, at any given time there were approximately 10 such churches.[12] They included such groups as Divine Healing Church of Christ, Åladura, Jehovah Nissi Healer's Temple, Church of the Savior, Church of Melchizedek, and the Wings of Bethany. Although there are a wide variety of founders and churches, the founders were generally, but not always, literate (4 of the 10 were illiterate); tended to be males (2 out of the 10 were female); almost all claimed to have experienced a prophetic vision that led them to establish a church or go into the ministry.

The Church of the Messiah, located on one of the main roads

11. For a detailed discussion of how this occurs in traditional religion, see Chapter III of Leith Mulling, Healing, Religion and Social Change in Southeastern Ghana, Unpublished Ph. D. dissertation, University of Chicago, 1975.

12. Research was conducted from 1970 to 1972. Although I did intensive research in the Church of the Messiah, I attended meetings and conducted interviews in the other spiritualist churches.

it joins Labadi with Accra city-center, had the largest membership of the spiritualist churches in Labadi. The congregation of approximately 1000 is, in a general sense, representative of all but the highest strata of the Labadi population (most of whom attended the "orthodox" churches). Women are present in greater proportions during the weekly meetings, with attendance at the Sunday meeting being approximately 60% women.[13] All age groups and most occupational categories are represented, with farmers, fishermen, wageworkers, petty traders, and clerks predominating. Although the majority of the membership is Labadian, there is a significant proportion of non-Labadian Gas (including the founder), as well as Africans of other ethnic groups. Church members, who refer to each other as "brother" or "sister" appear to socialize outside of the context of the church, to visit each other when sick and to exchange information about occupational and educational opportunities. The young people's group of 100 men and women between the ages of 18 and 25, participates in structured activities such as parties, games, and discussions.

The church hierarchy includes, in addition to the founder, an assistant pastor, "president," and the praying band, who assist the founder in ministering to the needs of the congregation. The founder, called "father" by the congregation, is a 30-year-old married man from Accra, who has two small daughters. After several years of schooling, he worked for the Department of Agriculture and as a part-time lay preacher. He claims that after experiencing a vision he decided to attend Bible College. He founded the church in Labadi in 1968 as a result of a breakaway from another spiritualist church in Accra. He has now founded three branches of the church in surrounding areas. The assistant pastor, who is the founder's mother's brother, is called "uncle" by the congregation. He has had no formal theological training. Five assistants were being trained by the founder; two of them are his brothers and one of the five is a woman who lives in the area of the church. Training is said to extend for a period of 3 years. The "president" of the church is the chairman of a loan association that makes loans to small businesses. In contrast to most members of the congregation, he appeared to be relatively wealthy— he owned several large houses and a large American car and was financing the studies of two young daughters in London and Germany. It was through the financial auspices of the president that the found-

---

13. In this respect, the Church of the Messiah was somewhat atypical in comparison with other churches in Labadi, which generally had a higher proportion of females.

er (who refers to the president as "father" although there is no biological relationship) made a tour of pentecostal churches in the United States. Members of the praying bands are considered to be elders of the church and take an active part in advising the congregation. The most senior (in terms of status) member is a non-Ga skilled worker in his forties, who is a supervisor of carpentry for the State Construction Corporation. The other members of the praying bank (eight in all) are either clerks or fairly successful market women.

The meeting, held three times a week, with Friday evening reserved for healing, is the major public ritual in the spiritualist churches. Although the Sunday morning meetings are usually filled to capacity, with people standing in the aisles and outside the church, weekday meetings are often only one-half to two-thirds filled. Meetings are usually conducted by the founder, the assistant pastor, or both, assisted by members of the praying band. The founder usually speaks in English (with simultaneous translation into Ga and Tshi) and occasionally speaks Ga; the assistant pastor, however, always speaks in Ga. Although occasional meetings are held elsewhere (e.g., on the beach), they usually take place in the "temple," a large rectangular cement building, roofed with corrugated iron. Outside the entrance to the building stands a cross; the interior is furnished with an altar—a symbol of power—a large picture of Jesus, and benches seating approximately 1000. Women, who are seated separately from the men, are required to wear a white head kerchief to all meetings and are sometimes asked to dress all in white.

Although meetings may vary according to type, there is a general outline to which all meetings conform. The ritual units involved in interaction always include the congregation (either as a whole or as individual members) and the leader of the meeting (who may be the founder or the assistant pastor). Singing, prayer, possession episodes, and a sermon occur at every meeting, although there is much flexibility with respect to the order of performance.

Singing: The meeting begins and ends with the singing of religious songs, some are Ghanaian in origin, others, translations of traditional European Christian hymns. During the service any member of the congregation may spontaneously begin a song, which will then be taken up by the entire congregation. This individual initiative contrasts significantly with the public rituals of traditonal religions where such roles are ascribed: songs and drumming are performed by specific individuals—elders, mediums, or priests, often representing lineages.

Prayer: Prayer, by the founder or congregation, for the congregation as a whole or for specific members, may occur at almost any point in the service. The entire congregation may be told to pray silently for their individual needs while focusing their eyes on the picture of Jesus. Individuals may voluntarily walk or be called to the altar for specific prayers by the founder, other visionaries in the church membership, or the entire congregation. The following invocation by the founder is fairly typical: "Everyone should get up and pray for this woman, taking her as your own daughter, your own sister, or your own friend . . . so that God may have mercy on her and deliver her from the traps that have been set for her by her enemies." Although each member of the congregation has the capacity to pray, and thus to secure blessings, the prayers of the founder, church officials, and praying band are thought to be most efficacious and therefore are most in demand.

Possession: Individuals may become possessed by the Holy Spirit at any point during the meeting, although predisposition toward possession appears to be related to the high level of tension that is generated during particularly significant points in the sermon when holy water is sprinkled on the congregation or when prayer is particularly intense. Possession may take a variety of forms, from mild convulsive movements of the upper half of the body to sporadic jerks, doubling the body from the waist. Glossolalia did not occur in this particular church. The significant point here is that although my data indicate that a small group (approximately 50) may be possessed occasionally, and the majority not at all, all individuals are thought to have the potential to become possessed. Again, this presents a contrast to public traditional religions, where only designated mediums of the gods become possessed.[14]

Sermon: The sermon is the central focus of the meeting and one of the main vehicles through which ideology is transmitted. Sermons vary in length, style, and content, but both the founder and the members of the congregation consider the sermon to be a source of information about proper and improper modes of behavior. Although the sermon is created and delivered by the founder or assistant pastor, the congregation actively participates, demonstrating approval and agreement through applause and interjection. For a 1 month period, I recorded all 12 sermons given. Analysis of them reveals that the following major themes occurred: (*a*) salvation (appeared in some form in every sermon); (*b*) the exhortation to abstain from traditional religious practices (8 sermons); (*c*) personal respon-

14. More recent forms of traditional religion include "democratic" possession cults (cf. Ranger 1972:12).

sibility for behavior (8 sermons); (*d*) admonition to place "the law of God" above that of one's forefathers (6 sermons); (*e*) exhortation not to envy the property of others, but to "trust God" or "lay up treasures in heaven rather than on earth" (6 sermons); (*f*) brotherly love for other Christians (5 sermons); (*g*) the shame of not being bred in a Christian household (2 sermons). My observations over the period of a year confirm the predominance of these themes.[15] The sermons, then, give information about desirable behavior and undesirable behavior. Undesirable behavior seems to be primarily associated with aspects of traditional society, and new orientations are presented as superior.

The overriding theme of most sermons is salvation. In attempting to delineate the indigenous meaning associated with salvation,[16] I found that although church members occasionally allude to otherworldly phenomena, most associate salvation with divine assistance in solving everyday problems of "unbeez" ("unbusiness" or unemployment), family relations, and health. This was not only my observation, but also that of the founder who noted "Here in spiritualist churches, most people come with the simple aim of acquiring something from the church—getting healed or getting their requests answered by the Lord." To the congregation, then, the importance of salvation concerns help with everyday problems. The Christian God is held to be the source of benevolent power that may be brought to bear on solving problems. The sermons tell the congregation how salvation, resulting in help with problems, can be achieved. This is often expressed in such concepts as the precedence of the "law of God" or "drawing away from the things of this world." Such concepts are often projected in the form of parables about conflicting loyalties in the family of a kinship group. One such sermon took as its central text a story about a domestic group, all of whom, except the youngest son, worshiped a traditional God. The father went to a traditional religious practitioner to see what could be done about improving his fortune. He was told that his circumstances would improve if his entire family were faithful to the traditional gods. As a result of this divination, the father requested the youngest

15. During the period of a year during which I attended at least one, and as many as three, meetings per week, I took detailed notes on the text of the sermon.

16. The English term "salvation" was often cited by members of the congregation as a reason for membership in the spiritualist church. Further questioning about the meaning of salvation always elicited discussion reflecting expectations of supernatural help with problems of this world. For church members, "salvation" appears to refer to a state of being: one that will bring blessings in the afterworld, but more important, will result in help with problems of this world.

son to stop going to church. Confronted with the dilemma of whether to obey the precepts of the Christian God or his father and his father's gods the boy decided that "the law of God is greater than the law of your father" and refused to stop attending church. The father attempted to have the son killed by an old woman; she accidentally killed the compliant firstborn son instead, and the Christian son was saved and the parents punished. The conclusion was greeted with enthusiastic applause by the congregation. This sort of parable is particularly significant in view of the strong orientation toward filial obedience in the traditional society.

Sermons often admonish church members to refrain from a variety of traditional relationships and practices. Foremost among these are those practices concerned with traditional religion, which are characterized as evil and dangerous; the Christian God is said to be the only source of protection:

> Jesus is the only one who can protect you from the witches, fetish priests, *ju-ju* men, men who put something down for you to walk on. All these things are all around you and only Jesus can protect you. In these evil days, you may eat with someone and your hand crosses and she will have some medicine in her hand that will harm you. Do not take anything from anyone [From author's fieldnotes].

Note that the last sentence suggests a mode of behavior that is in direct opposition to the reciprocal relationships of traditional society.

The doctrinal insistence on the exclusiveness of the Christian God has frequently been cited as one of the distinguishing features of the transition to Christianity (cf. Horton 1971). This contrasts with the attitudes of practitioners of traditional religion who have historically been very tolerant of other religions, often adding foreign powers to the pantheon and acknowledging the Christian God as the supreme being of traditional religion. Their attitude toward Christians is usually one of amused tolerance. However, although Christians often solicit treatment from traditional practitioners, the exclusiveness of the Christian God is one of the basic tenets propounded in the spiritualist church.

The themes of rejection of traditional gods and exclusive participation in Christianity are often combined with emphasis on each individual's responsibility for achieving his own salvation. The individual is often posed in opposition to the world:

> So far as you have loved the world for some reason; then it is enmity with God. . . But if you think of the world and say to yourself that I

could neither leave this thing or that thing, this person or that. . .
leave everything and come to the Lord so that victory will be yours.
[From author's field notes].

Unemployment (or the desire to improve one's occupational
category), given by both the founder and the congregation as a major
reason for church membership, is a frequent topic of reference in
sermons as well as in individual requests. The related subjects of employment, wealth, and prestige are often involved in contradictory
motifs. The congregation is often charged to work hard and admonished not to be lazy (cf. Weber 1930): "If you do not have a job,
will your younger sisters and brothers respect you?" At the same
time it is recognized that the high level of unemployment in Ghana is
not the fault of the individual, and the unemployed and marginally
employed are instructed to have faith. The members of the congregation, many of whose status is somewhat marginal, are comforted
with the exhortation that the Christian way is not to love money or
to be envious of the wealth or possessions of others, but to concern
one's self with otherworldly rewards. The use of these themes is il-
lustrated in the following sermon. The founder recounted the story
of the laying on of hands and the descent of the Holy Spirit unto the
Apostles, emphasizing the fact that the Spirit could not be purchased
with money which is "the source of all evil." The founder reiterated
the theme of the sermon: "the Bible tells us that we must lay up our
treasure in heaven, and not be jealous of the suit, the shoes, the
cloth, the necklaces and the shoes that others have and you do not,
because .these are worldly things and they will pass away." He then
recounted a story about a poor man who was employed by a rich
man. While the poor man was farming the rich man's land, he discovered a locked box. Although the rich man had never seen the box
before, he confiscated it, insisting that it was his property. (At this
point the founder interjected, "Selfishness!") When the poor man
contested the ownership of the box, the chief decided that the box
would belong to whomever could bring him a key that would open
it. The rich man, who bribed the caretaker of the box and had a key
made, claimed the box by virtue of the fact that he had a key. When
the box was opened and found to contain the head of the chief's
missing daughter, the rich man was punished by death. The congregation was admonished to take a lesson from this, not to be jealous of
the property of others. The congregation actively participated, expressing disapproval of the tactics of the rich man, applauding his
downfall, and expressing agreement with the opening and concluding
remarks of the sermon.

A number of themes are interwoven in this sermon. Implicit in the formulation that money is the source of all evil is the recognition of the money-centered economy, unequal access to resources, and its destructive effect on traditional relationships. The reaction of the congregation as well as the interjections of the founder indicate some hostility toward the unequal relationship between the rich and the poor man and a recognition that property is often acquired by exploitation of the poor, bribery, and corruption. This is seen as a negative aspect of social relations, yet the unequal relations are rationalized by the conclusion of the sermon: "Do not be jealous of someone's property, because if you follow it you will surely die one day. Let us lay up our treasures in heaven, but the rich man laid his on earth."

Brotherly love is a frequent motif. Members of the church are continually exhorted to help and love one another, placing associations of Christian fellowship above those of the lineage. Although this church was predominantly Ga, members of other ethnic groups attended as well. An Easter sermon instructed the congregation that all people, regardless of their ethnic group, are brothers in Christ, as long as they belong to the Christian community: "A Mossi-man is your brother. How many of you would sit down to supper with a Daga-man? He is your brother in Christ."

While prayer, singing, possession, and the sermon occur at every meeting, there is no set order in which they must be performed, and additional elements may be added at the discretion of the founder. Members of the congregation may be anointed with water or oil that has been sacralized by the prayers of the founder. Lighting of candles may play a prominent part in the meeting. On one such occasion the congregation was told to bring white candles to the evening meeting. The candles were collected, prayed over, and redistributed. The founder, assistant pastor, and members of the praying band walked through the room lighting the candles of the congregation with their own. Amid singing and praying, the candles were then raised to face level and each person extinguished the candle of the person sitting next to him, creating an ambience of intimacy and solidarity among the members of the church.

Offerings of money are collected at every meeting. At least once, and sometimes twice during a meeting, at a signal from the founder, the congregation forms a line and dances past the collection plate, dropping offerings into it. Although I was not able to verify how much money is collected and how it is spent, the founder's claim that most people can afford to give only a few pesewas[17] seems reasonable in view of the financial circumstances of the majority of the members. However, the offering taken during the meeting is not the only source of income. Clients who feel that the founder has been instrumental in healing or helping them may make a special contribution. Candles, incense, and holy water used in healing may be sold. The congregation may cooperate in special projects involving money. For example, members of the congregation were urged to invest 40 pesewas a month for the first month and 30 pesewas per month for 6 months, in order to insure that there would be money to bury them if they died. On one occasion, a man had died but had not contributed enough money for the church to bury him. The founder took the opportunity to admonish the members of the congregation to keep up their payments. I was told by a member of the praying band that some members of the church did not have families to bury them: "We are their brothers and sisters."

A major concern of many African Christian churches is healing. This observation led Baeta (1962:47) to describe spiritualist churches in Ghana as "being preoccupied with the practice of faith-healing almost to the exclusion of any other interests." It was certainly the case that problems thought to require healing were most prevalent in the Church of the Savior. My perusal of the consultation record for a random week in three different months indicated that in each week at least two-thirds of the clients came to be healed. In all cases of consultation for spiritual healing that I witnessed, the patient came alone or with one friend or relative. Official representatives of the lineage did not participate in any capacity. The problem was recounted to the healer by the patient; the healer made a diagnosis immediately or suggested that the patient return in a few days, after which the cause of the illness would be revealed through prayer, visions, and dreams. The founder or assistant pastor would inform the patient of the cause of the illness privately or during the healing meeting. When the illness was thought to be "supernaturally" caused, the diagnosis usually given to the patient was witchcraft, and less frequently, sorcery, both of which are thought to be manifestations of the devil. Unlike the traditional healer, the spiritualist healer rarely identified specific relationships thought to be problematic. In some cases individuals were warned to leave their lineage house and to sleep in the church building. Prescribed treatment consisted of the

17. In 1970-1972, one pesewa was equivalent to one cent (U.S.).

repetition of the psalms and prayers, burning of candles, and bathing with holy water. All these activities could be performed by the patient in private. Patients were usually advised to confess their sins, to participate in the public meeting, to become a member of the church if they had not done so already, and to solicit the prayers of the founder and praying band.

The following case of a 30-year-old market woman exemplifies typical features of diagnosis and treatment in the spiritualist church.

> A is the mother of eight children and has had no formal schooling. Before her illness she resided in a lineage house, but at the advice of the founder, she remained in the church building for treatment. Three months ago, she began to complain of general malaise, fatigue, and weight loss. Although she considered herself to be a Presbyterian, after several unsuccessful visits to the hospital, she consulted the founder of the Church of the Savior (where her sister was a member). Upon consultation, the founder told her that his vision revealed that there was witchcraft in her lineage house to which she was vulnerable. Her treatment regime included residence at the church building, attendance at all the meetings, repetition of prayers and psalms, the lighting of candles, and prayer by the founder, assistant pastor and members of the praying band all of which were expected to strengthen her and enable her to withstand the effects of witchcraft. After approximately one month, at a public meeting, she declared to the congregation that her symptoms had disappeared, giving thanks and vowing to be faithful. After her discharge, she decided not to return to her lineage house, but to live alone with her children in an individual house. [From author's fieldnotes].

IV

The relationship between the spiritualist church and the emerging social structure is overt in the sense that the church, in its function as a small business enterprise, incorporates the relationships of individual enterprise that characterize the new socioeconomic order and has the potential to provide access to wealth and prestige for the founder. On a more subtle level (particularly for the congregation) is the fact that spiritualist religion ritually reproduces and thus rationalizes these new social relationships. We have noted that the emerging social structure in Ghana has been characterized by the decline of the lineage as a collective wealth-holding unit and the proliferation of individual small-scale enterprise. Spiritualist churches, in a sense, may be seen to function as small businesses: most founders seem to have expectations that the church will become a fairly lucrative enterprise that will allow them a certain degree of upward mobility and prestige.[18] Although the offering alone may not facilitate this expectation, there are additional avenues of income. Founders who attain a reputation for success, particularly at healing, may achieve a measure of prestige, attracting influential church members; in this way the founders are often able to obtain sponsors who may help them to expand their enterprise and influence. We have noted that the founder of the Church of the Savior was able to obtain the backing of the church president, an influential businessman who financed the founder's travels abroad. This trip to the United States not only resulted in contact with U.S.-based Pentecostal groups that were in a position to render concrete moral and financial support, but also increased his prestige in Ghana, which could, in turn, bring him more wealthy and influential clients. Another source of income and prestige for the founder is the training of new practitioners.

The small business aspect of spiritualist churches is recognized by the townspeople of Labadi, who frequently verbalized their belief that most founders are in the church solely for the purpose of making money. This sentiment was expressed most graphically during the annual traditional religious ritual, particularly the aspect that involves the spontaneous composition of songs about people and events of the previous year. Several of these songs concerned founders of various spiritualist churches, who were said to be interested primarily in making money. Among spiritualist church-going population, this belief takes the form that the founders of *other* spiritualist churches are primarily concerned with the financial aspect.

In Labadi, spiritualist churches seem to follow the pattern of the majority of small businesses and enterprises: a few are successful, but most are transient. The spiritualist churches are not the only religious institutions to reflect the emerging entrepreneurial relations. Growing commercialization characterizes many traditional practitioners—"medicine-owners" and spirit mediums who have set up private practices, see clients on an individual basis, and train apprentices for remuneration. However, despite a similar pattern of commerciali-

---

18. Owusu (1970: 109–110) has remarked on the relationship between spiritualist churches and small businesses in Ghana:

> clearheaded people primarily interested in making money establish churches the way others set up businesses. Ostensibly the sects and separatist churches are there to show votaries the true way to the "everlasting kingdom" and salvation . . . however, as a few skeptics admit, they are a major source of income and power for the founders.

zation, spiritualist Christianity differs from traditional religion in its overt identification with a new structure.

For the congregation, then, while participation in the spiritualist church does not represent an avenue for individual enterprise in the form of a business as it does for the founder, Christianity, unlike traditional religion, is identified with the more desirable status positions in the new stratification structure. We have noted that there is a high level of aspiration to the rapidly growing middle stratum of clerks, managers, and bureaucrats. Christianity, unlike traditional religion, is associated with both the formal education and the informal values and modes of behavior that are prerequisites to attaining these statuses. From the opening of the first official workshop for training skilled laborers by the Basel Mission, formal education has always been closely associated with Christianity. In Labadi, the three major schools continue to be associated with the Anglican, Presbyterian, and Methodist Churches. Although the spiritualist churches do not usually have formal schools connected to them, formal and informal learning and exchange take place. Through the general meeting or through more specific vehicles such as the young peoples' group, not only are networks established through which information about work and educational opportunities may be exchanged, but new modes of behavior and new orientations are also projected.

These ideological orientations stand in opposition to those of traditional society; ritual and belief in the spiritualist church enact and reproduce relationships relevant to the changing social unit. Unlike traditional religion, where the individual never consititutes a ritual unit but is submerged in the lineage, spiritualist Christianity differentiates the individual.[19] Whereas public traditional religion stresses egalitarianism, complementarity, and kinship obligations, the spiritualist church celebrates individual initiative and rationalizes inequality. This contrast is apparent in the ritual of the meeting and most evident in the ideology of the sermon and the practices surrounding healing. In the major public ritual, the meeting, the congre-

---

19. Several scholars have noted that the trend toward individualization appears to be characteristic of the Christianization of African societies. Bastide (1966:470) remarks, "Christianity in effect brings to people who think in terms of 'We' rather than 'I,' a condemnation of the 'We' concept." In discussing religion and the transformation of African societies, Wilson (1971:21) examines the concept of the individual in the New Testament:

> In the new Testament the worth of every individual is repeatedly asserted, and the history of the Christian Church has in part been a history of how individual worth was cherished. At the Reformation the stress was on each man judging for himself, on the freedom of individual conscience, and on individual responsibility.

gation may be seen to constitute one pole of ritual interaction and the individual the other. The congregation constitutes a very different unit from that associated with traditional religions: the relationship between members of the group is no longer based on kinship ties, neither in the narrow sense of the lineage nor in the broader sense of the town. Although kinship may be a function of some areas of interaction (for example, the assistant pastor and founder are mothers' brothers), blood ties no longer constitute the basis of action. The fact that the inclusive social unit being ritualized is no longer based on lineage groups but rather refers to a wider unit is significant in the context of the broadening scale of social relationships. Although there were extensive relationships between ethnic groups before the European intrusion, interactions between ethnic groups involving work, residence, and marriage now occur on an everyday basis. The widening scope of relationships is sacralized in repeated admonitions toward brotherly love. The extent to which the spiritualist churches in some countries were instrumental in consolidating divergent groups, developing national or class awareness, and organizing to deal with the effects of colonialism may be seen as one of the "unintended" effects of colonialism. Although members of the Church of the Savior assume some collective responsibility for each other, the major share of responsibility rests with the individual. This is evident in the previously cited example of investment for coffins—the church will bury its members, but each must have invested the price of the coffin.[20]

Thus, at the same time that the congregation emerges as the symbol of a wider social group, the individual is differentiated. Perhaps the differentiation of the individual from prior social groups is a prerequisite not only to stratification, but as Mintz (1974) suggests, to the development of a wider class consciousness. Nevertheless, we find that in the ritual elements of the public meeting, although the congregation participates as a group in singing, dancing, and praying, it is individual members acting solely according to their own predelictions who start a song, begin a dance, utter a prophecy, become possessed, or request healing. Although activities undertaken in the context of the congregation are thought to be especially efficacious, individuals do not represent units crucial to the success of the ritual. This presents a contrast to the public rituals of traditional religion where all roles are ascribed on the basis of lineage membership and

---

20. This contrasts with traditional practices where responsibility for funeral provisions rested with the major lineage.

seniority; the major rituals cannot be successfully completed without the presence of the representatives of all lineage groups, symbolizing the complementarity and interdependence of social units. In the spiritualist church, on the other hand, many of the ritual activities are basically subjective (e.g., prayer and recitation of psalms) and can be performed by any individual without the presence of a social group; each individual is responsible for his or her own salvation. Although each member of the congregation may perform ritual activities individually, the founder, and to some extent other members of the church hierarchy, have a more central role in public worship. By virtue of their control over the content of the sermons, their interpretation of visions, or the fact that their prayers are thought to be more efficacious, they occupy a special position as "elder" and thus the main interpreters of values. Unlike traditional religion, where "elder" is a status based upon chronological age and generational position, the elder of the church obtains that status through achieved prestige. Both the members of the hierarchy and the congregation phrase the requirements of seniority and prestige in terms of the individual's closeness to divinity as evidenced in effectiveness of prayer, efficacy of prophecy, and purity of life. However, when we examine the life-styles of the senior church members, it appears that the achievement of certain statuses and a degree of material prosperity is taken as a significant indication of the individual's successful relationship with God and worthiness of respect—we have noted that the president is a successful businessman, and the senior males and females are skilled workers, clerks, or successful market women. Central roles in worship, then, rather than being determined by the complementary rotation of the lineages and being based on generational and lineage position, are determined by factors such as successful individual enterprise, education, and literacy, reflecting and reproducing the hierarchical structure of the wider society.

Although the members of the church hierarchy may exercise a degree of control over the interpretation of what constitutes salvation, personal salvation is held to be the responsibility of individual members of the congregation. As we have noted, for most members of the congregation, it is hoped that "salvation" will bring very concrete results—a job, or help with problems of family, kinship, or health. Salvation, however, is not automatically available to members of the congregation: it is predicated on adherence to particular modes of behavior. These may be communicated to members of the congregation during visions, of members of the hierarchy, or through the prayers of the praying band, but are explicated more directly and explicitly during the sermon. Condensed in the tenets of "faith," "salvation," and exclusive adherence to the "'law of God" are new priorities, new modes of behavior, and new values that take precedence over old ones. Most significant is the abnegation of the basic principles of the essentially egalitarian kin-based society and the emphasis on individual responsibility and the rationalization of inequality, particularly manifested in instructions not to envy the property of others but to concern one's self with "the things of the Lord."

Healing rituals play a key role in transmitting and establishing these new ideological precepts; it is, perhaps, the inclusion of such "traditional" activities as healing that make the spiritualist churches more effective (at least in terms of numbers) than the "orthodox" churches. Because of the profound significance of health and well-being for the individual, the meanings, proscriptions, and underlying symbols utilized in healing become particularly influential. Specific goals and values may be explicitly stated or implicitly communicated as prerequisites for regaining health. It is reasonable to suggest that the dependent state and the need for help render the individual particularly vulnerable to this form of suggestion; acceptance of premises upon which healing is predicated is understood as necessary for successful healing.[21]

Spiritualist and traditional healing have some similarities of form, but differ significantly in their content. While traditional healing attempts to restructure lineage relationships, thus reinforcing the lineage as a social unit, spiritualist healing emphasizes the individuation of the patient. Both types of healing include phases of divination and treatment in which the cause of illness is first identified and then neutralized or eliminated. In both types of healing, forces external to the individual—usually witchcraft and sorcery, are thought to be instrumental causes of illness. It is with respect to the ultimate explanation of illness, however, that the contrast between the two systems becomes most evident. Unlike traditional healing, where the ultimate explanation for why an illness has occurred is sought in the relationship between the individual and the group, divination in the spiritualist church in seeking to reveal the reason for which the individual is open to malevolent forces, often finds the ultimate cause to be internal to the individual—often phrased as lack of faith or salvation. In the final analysis, the illness is the responsibility of the individual, to be overcome through increased "faith." Treatment,

21. This has also been noted by Turner (1967) and Kennedy (1973).

then, is directed toward strengthening the individual through ritual activities that are basically individual and subjective—lighting candles, burning incense, saying prayers and psalms, and bathing in holy water. Not only is there no attempt to reconstruct disrupted lineage relationships, but frequently the founder encourages the discontinuity of these relationships as an aspect of treatment. The pressure to withdraw from these relationships is augmented by the prohibition against participating in any aspect of traditional religions, as well as encouragement to move out of the lineage house temporarily or permanently. Unlike the public rituals of traditonal healing where attendance of lineage members is required if they are not to incur suspicion of guilt, members of the lineage have no role in spiritualist healing. Unlike traditional healing, responsibility for one member's misfortune is not shared by others; neither will the individual be held responsible for the actions of his kinsmen. The success of treatment, then, is thought to be dependent on increasing the strength of the individual through acceptance of the implicit or explicit values that are transmitted through healing rituals. While both traditional and spiritualist healing seek to impress certain perspectives and orientations on the patient, they pose very different solutions to the problem of illness. Whereas the goal of traditional healing is to repair and restructure relationships based on the premises of the village community, the goal of spiritualist healing is to reinforce the individual, often by removing him from his kin, and impress upon him the necessity of salvation: the acceptance of new values, symbolized in the concept of "faith."

I have suggested that an important aspect of the Church of the Savior is the rationalization and reinforcement of the new relationships, characterized by increasing individualization. The fact that these elements occur in a context of cultural continuity differentiates spiritualist churches from "orthodox" churches and makes them more effective vehicles for the transmission of new ideologies. The church functions as an arena in which traditional cultural elements are subsumed, reworked and given new meanings that are relevant to the new social relationships. It is, perhaps, with respect to these continuities that all African Christian churches may be called "nationalist" in the cultural sense. While all such movements did not function in the political arena to promote independence, all embody the reworking of African cultural elements. Continuities of such features as spirit possession, musical forms, polygamy, and healing are apparent to the casual observer. Witchcraft and sorcery continue to function as idioms for citing causes of illness. Old symbols occur in a new context, retaining the indigenous explanation and associated meanings. For example, the color white, used in traditional religion for facial markings and for the robes of priests and elders, now appears in the dress of worshippers and in white candles burned to cure illness. Thus white retains its connotation of efficacy; water and oil, used for anointment in both traditional religion and Christianity, continue to symbolize divinity. New symbols are often utilized in a manner similar to old ones. The placement of the cross in the courtyard of the spiritualist healer is reminiscent of the *otutuu,* a representation of traditional powers that stands in the courtyard of every traditional healer to ward off evil powers. Many of the elements are traditional but their contemporary configuration refers to emerging relationships.

In discussing the relationship between social change and an African Christian church in Labadi, I have suggested that the development of stratification by class, characterized by increasing individualization is particularly significant to the emergence of this religious form. The spiritualist church not only embodies these new relationships in its function as a small business, but also symbolizes or reproduces them on a ritual level. While I have emphasized the congruence with the emerging structure of stratification, I am not suggesting that spiritualist Christianity strains toward functional integration. It is obvious from the data that it incorporates diverse and contradictory elements. Included in its ideology are the views of different strata: we find, on one hand, sympathy with the problems of unemployment, inequality, and social injustice, on the other, the declaration that the solution is not to be found on earth, but in heaven. It includes the relationships of colonial domination embodied in the European colonial thrust, but also the reaction against it evident in the awareness of a common position and the potential for nationalist organization. Within structural limitations a range of possibilities[22] is available, as is evidenced by the fact that some churches functioned as political movements and others did not. Spiritualist religion, then, both interprets new relationships and instills in the individual a commitment to action (cf. Geertz 1966). However, following in the tradition of Marx, I suggest that spiritualist Christianity took hold because of the existence of specific relationships that make it relevant: basic to urbanization, demographic changes, and other changes in scale, was emerging class stratification.

22. I have emphasized the structural configuration of the ideological elements; the selection and utilization of relevant elements by the individual, within structural limitations, is the subject of another paper.

REFERENCES

Baeta, C. G. 1962 *Prophetism in Ghana.* London: S. C. M. Press.

Bastide, R. 1966 "Messianism and Economic and Social Development," In *Social Change: The Colonial Situation,* I. Wallerstein, Ed. New York: John Wiley and Sons.

Geertz, C. 1966 "Religion as a Cultural System" in M. Banton *Anthropological Approaches to the Study of Religion.* Tavistock ASA.

Jahoda, G. 1966 "Social Aspirations, Magic and Witchcraft: In *The New Elites of Tropical Africa.* P. C. Lloyd, Ed. London: Oxford University Press.

Kennedy, J. 1973 "Cultural Psychiatry," In *Handbook of Social and Cultural Anthropology.* John Honigman, Ed. Chicago. Rand-McNally and Company.

Kilson, M. 1971 *Kpele Lala: Ga Religious Songs and Symbols.* Cambridge: Harvard University Press.

Kimble, D. 1963 *A Political History of Ghana.* Oxford: Clarendon Press.

Mintz, S. 1974 "The Rural Proletariat and the Problem of Rural Proletarian Consciousness." *The Journal of Peasant Studies* 1: 291-325.

Mullings, L. 1975. Healing, Religion and Social Change in Southeastern Ghana. Unpublished Ph D. Dissertation, University of Chicago.

Opoku, K.A. 1970. A Brief History of Independent Church Movements in Ghana 1862-1960. Unpublished paper.

Owusu, M. 1970. *Uses and Abuses of Political Power.* Chicago: University of Chicago Press.

Peel, J.D.Y. 1968. *Aladura: A Religious Movement among the Yoruba.* London.

Ranger, T.O. 1972. "Introduction" in *The Historical Study of African Religion.* T. O. Ranger and I. Kimambo, Eds. Berkeley: University of California Press.

Szereszewski, R. 1975. *Structural Changes in the Economy of Ghana, 1891-1911.* London: Weidenfeld and Nicolson.

Turner, V. 1967. *The Forest of Symbols.* New York: Cornell University Press.

Weber, M. 1930 *The Protestant Ethic and the Spirit of Capitalism.* London: George Allen and Unwin, Ltd.

Wilson, M. 1969. *Religion and the Transformation of Society.* Cambridge: Cambridge University Press.

III
Walton Johnson

THE AFRICANIZATION
OF A MISSION CHURCH
The African Methodist
Episcopal Church in Zambia

The African Methodist Episcopal (A.M.E.) Church was founded in 1816 in Philadelphia, formed by the coalescence of a number of black American congregations which had broken away from white Methodist Episcopal churches. It was subsequently promoted by a small, free black intelligentsia in Philadelphia, Baltimore, New York, and Charleston. In breaking away from the white bodies, they were protesting growing racial schism in the churches and in the broader society.

An early forerunner of the church, and a precursor of one of its principal social roles, was the Free Africa Society established in Philadelphia in 1787. This mutual aid society was formed by Richard Allen in the first instance of blacks separating themselves from a white congregation. Significantly, the religious character of the organization was submerged and its efforts were concentrated on caring for the sick, homeless, and dead.

Put succinctly, then, the A.M.E. church in America was founded by an urbanizing black elite, in conditions of heightening ethnic pluralism, and it quickly adopted an important social role in the black community (Singleton 1952; DuBois 1899; Johnson 1977).

89

AFRICAN CHRISTIANITY
Patterns of Religious Continuity

After having established congregations in West Africa when Daniel Coker emigrated to Sierra Leone in 1820 and having begun formal missionary activity to West Africa in the 1870s, the A.M.E. church became established in southern Africa in 1896, when the Ethiopian church amalgamated with it. The Ethiopian church was formed in Pretoria in 1892 as a reaction to increasing discrimination in the Wesleyan Methodist church of southern Africa. By 1896, the young church had expanded to include 70 ministers and 2800 members and thus was beginning to cause alarm in white circles. In the meantime, through contacts with South Africans studying at the A.M.E. university in Wilberforce, Ohio, the leaders of the Ethiopean Church had become acquainted with the A.M.E. church in the United States. They decided to amalgamate with the A.M.E. partly in the hope that ties with the Americans would help protect their church from the hostile mission churches and the white governments (Coan 1961; Roux 1964; Flournoy 1976; Johnson 1978).

Despite the exodus of a major segment of the membership to form the Order of Ethiopia, the A.M.E. church was quickly established in the Cape, Orange River, and Transvaal colonies. Also, carried by the substantial African migration to and from employment opportunities, the church spread to Basutoland (1903), Southern Rhodesia (1900), Bechuanaland (1901), Swaziland (1904), and later to Nyasaland (1924).

By 1903, it had also reached Barotseland in Northern Rhodesia where the activities of its leader, Willie Mokalapa, caused considerable concern in political and missionary circles. Willie Mokalapa was a Suto pastor who had originally gone to Barotseland as an evangelist with the Paris Missionary Society, under the leadership of the well-known French missionary, François Coillard. Several reports state that, after working 10 years with Coillard, Mokalapa and some of his colleagues became agitated by the discriminatory policy in the Paris Missionary Society concerning pay and conditions and that Mokalapa withdrew his allegiance after quarreling with Coillard over these matters (Favre 1913; Ranger 1965; Johnson 1977).

In 1903 Mokalapa was appointed A.M.E. Presiding Elder for Barotseland and he returned to establish a mission there. In this new endeavor, he was encouraged and actively assisted by the Lozi administration. He built a large station a few miles from Lealui and had a large and enthusiastic congregation. One of the nephews of Paramount Chief Lewanika and many of the sons of smaller chiefs joined the church.

Because the influence of Coillard's mission was greatly reduced, the French missionaries and the British South Africa Company did all in their power to prevent Mokalapa from continuing. In 1904 the Administration issued Proclamation 19 which it used to prevent A.M.E. missionaries and teachers, other than Mokalapa, from entering or reentering the country. At the same time, it actively tried to persuade the Lozi not to follow the A.M.E. However, the Lozi aristocracy supported Mokalapa because of dissatisfaction with education in the Paris Missionary Society School. The A.M.E. school, by contrast, promised to teach English, mathematics, and other subjects that could "assist in the modernization of Lozi society." It was also apparent to the Lozi that Mokalapa and his missionaries were genuinely interested in the progress of the Barotse nation. Coillard's mission was too closely associated with outside interests.

Despite the factors in its favor, Mokalapa's work was not successful. In 1904, he was sent by King Lewanika to Capetown to purchase several river boats and carts. He was accompanied by Lewanika's half brother and they carried £700 of state funds. In Capetown they were advised by the Reverend Henry Attaway of the A.M.E. church to patronize certain auctioneers to whom £636 was paid with the assurance that the goods would be sent along later. The river boats and carts never arrived at Lealui. Forced to return to Capetown to inquire into the matter, Mokalapa discovered that the auctioneers had gone bankrupt and that the money had been lost.

It is not clear what happened to Mokalapa after this. He did not return to Barotseland and the church never recovered from his absence. Several A.M.E. missionaries remained in Lealui until 1906 and Lewanika actively campaigned for more A.M.E. teachers, even suggesting that the British South Africa Company Administration pay their salaries. But the church withered and died as a result of the administration's prohibition on more A.M.E. teachers and missionaries entering the territory.

The church reappeared in Northern Rhodesia in 1930 amid industrial expansion on the Copperbelt. In 1924, the British colonial administration had assumed responsibility for governing the country. During the period that followed, the substantial increase in mining activity led to the growth of a number of new urban centers. Large numbers of Africans were brought from their village communities and placed as laborers in the money economy. In 1924 there were only 1300 Africans employed on the Copperbelt, but by 1930 there were nearly 22,000. At the same time, the white population also expanded rapidly, responding to industry's need for skilled and semi-skilled labor. During the 1924–1930 period, the number of whites on the Copperbelt grew from 4000 to 13,000, with most bringing harsh racial attitudes with them from South Africa. (Hall 1965).

Thus the prevailing social conditions in Northern Rhodesia were characterized by rapid urbanization and heightened racial schism, the same ingredients that were present when the A.M.E. church began in the United States and South Africa. The Africanization of the A.M.E. church in this context was its adaptation to the special needs of the African urban community.

The decades of the 1930s and 1940s were years of expansion for the church. During the early 1930s, it became one of the largest and most active Christian denominations on the Copperbelt. By 1933, there were A.M.E. congregations in Livingstone, Kalomo, Choma, Mazabuka, Mapanza, Monze, Lusaka, Mumbwa, Namwala, Broken Hill, Ndola, Kitwe, Mufulira, Luanshya, Fort Jameson, Kawambwa, and in rural villages in the Northern and Luapula provinces. Recalling the mood of that period, one person explained, "There was great excitement about having a church which belonged to Africa. They brought cattle and other goods. The people gave gifts and made sacrifices. . . . It was the people's first time to see an African minister. He was like Jesus."

The carriers of the church were themselves African. On the one hand, church officials and civil servants from Southern Rhodesia, Nyasaland, and South Africa brought the church to Northern Rhodesia and constituted its early leadership. On the other hand, Northern Rhodesian miners, clerks, and businessmen, in their movement throughout the country, started new congregations in virtually all of the towns and in some villages. Indeed, it is the presence of African initiative and indigenous leadership in the propagation of the A.M.E. church that gives it a character similar to African Christian movements which have originated on the continent.

During the period of accelerated social change, the demand for education among Africans was very great. The missions were looked to by all to provide schools since the colonial administration gave little attention to meeting the African's educational needs. As early as 1925, the Reverend H.M. Phiri applied to the government of Northern Rhodesia to build an A.M.E. school near Fort Jameson. In 1932, the A.M.E. church operated one of the two schools for Africans in Luanshya. It was primarily a night school where English was taught but it also gave some instruction in ordinary classroom subjects up to Standard I. About that same time, the A.M.E. was trying to establish a school near Mporokoso. It is likely that there were more schools sponsored by A.M.E. congregations during the church's early days in the country, but government records are inadequate on this point as are the A.M.E. records.

It is significant that the largest growth points for the church outside of the urban areas, where it had other social functions, were in those places where the schools were successful. In the Northern and Luapula provinces, for instance, there were three A.M.E. schools by 1942—one at Chiyanga, one at Chilwa, and one at Chipwa. They were primary schools founded by the Reverend J.L.C. Membe. Chilwa school was the largest, having four teachers and approximately 400 students. Chiyanga had three teachers and about 316 students. The Chipwa school had two teachers and about 117 students.

Another of the church's rural growth points was in the Kalomo-Choma area where Nachula school was located. The A.M.E. mission at Nachula was established in 1932 by the Reverend J. Marumo. Nachula was a primary school which concentrated on the teaching of English and arithmetic. As a result of Marumo's active missionary work, the church and school grew rapidly and the government received applications prior to 1940, for more than half a dozen smaller schools in the nearby villages. Many of the smaller schools failed owing to lack of funds.

In the mid-1940s there were seven A.M.E. schools in Northern Rhodesia—one at Mwinilunga, with two teachers; one at Mulungushi, with one teacher; one at Nachula, with one teacher; one at Molebatsi, with two teachers; one at Chisanga, with two teachers. The schools, however, did not receive regular support from the Annual Conference or the Episcopal District. Normally they were financed by the local congregations, with the pastors contributing from their meager resources. Most of the schools eventually failed owing to lack of funds to pay the recurrent expenses of teachers' salaries or the inability to meet the government requirements. Mission schools of other denominations were able to survive primarily because of the grants-in-aid and other support they received from the government. The A.M.E. church schools did not receive grants-in-aid because they did not have certified teachers and because the government's policy was "to discourage schools belonging to this denomination." Funds were not forthcoming from the church in the United States, so the schools eventually languished.

With regard to health facilities, records indicate that there has been only one A.M.E.-sponsored clinic. The Reverend J.M. Mubita, who was appointed to Namitome in Barotseland, started a clinic at his home in 1952 with drugs provided by the Provincial Medical Officer. In 1958, the Reverend Mubita purchased another house to use as a clinic and made grants to it to help its operations. The clinic continued functioning until 1962, when the government insisted that the A.M.E. church pay some fees in return for the medications and salaries it supplied. Neither the Annual Conference nor the Episcopal District provided these funds so Namitome Clinic was closed down.

The list of social service facilities begun by A.M.E. ministers can probably never be completed. Since most of them were purely local efforts, there was often no record of them. Indeed, the Annual Conference or Episcopal District was never able to take the responsibility for establishing social service facilities. The best they could do was to give funds occasionally to those projects that had begun locally. The inability of the church to continue providing schools and clinics diminished its attractiveness in the eyes of local people.

During the period of 1955 to 1960, the church also suffered from the absence of a trained ministry. Knowledge of English and the acquisition of secondary education became symbols of accomplishment and status and became more indispensable to life in Northern Rhodesia. Due to the absence of training opportunities, the A.M.E. ministry gradually slipped from the vanguard of emerging African talent to a position where it attracted many men who did not have the ability to succeed in other professions. Increasingly, the church did not attract the bright young men because it did not provide opportunities for higher education and because it offered no financial security. Consequently, most circuits were poorly administered and the church was hurt by maladministration.

Despite the absence of social service facilities and a trained ministry, 1945–1960 were still years of growth in membership, because the racial and political circumstances of Northern Rhodesia continued to give the A.M.E. church, as an African-controlled church, some advantages vis-a-vis most other denominations. At this time the white minority was pressing to institutionalize its privilege further. Economically, Africans were exploited. Socially, they were segregated. And politically, stratagems, such as the Central African Federation, were designed to protect white hegemony.

But in the early 1960s, as the Northern Rhodesian society changed and as the policies of the other churches changed, the A.M.E. church was thrust into a relatively poor position. The church's main attracting attributes, as we shall see, had been providing opportunities for leadership and authority, relating positively to African nationalism, providing the functions of an adaptive institution, and helping to meet the need for new forms of social organization in the urbanized society. It performed these functions at a time when few other institutions did so—thus making it distinctive and enhancing its appeal. However, during the 1960s, these attributes became increasingly shared by other institutions within the society. No longer being distinctive, the A.M.E.'s weaknesses with regard to trained ministry and social service facilities relegated it to a poor position in terms of mass appeal. The result of the church's failure to correct its weaknesses is that today it is declining.

According to figures of the parent church, in 1975 the church in Zambia had 96 congregations with a membership of about 15,000. However, an accurate membership figure is difficult to obtain. Some local estimates put the membership in excess of 25,000. Whatever the exact figure, the church now has congregations in all sections of Zambia, but is still heavily concentrated in the urban areas and in the rural areas of the Northern and Luapula Provinces.

In the 1970s the synchronic picture of the A.M.E. church is of a multiethnic, multinational, multilingual church composed of middle-aged and older people. Its educational standard, rate of literacy in English, and income levels are low. It is no longer the church of Zambia's elite. The diachronic picture is of a slowly dying church—a church which attracted members in greatest numbers during the 1940s and early 1950s but which, since the 1960s, has been losing its appeal.

II

The A.M.E. church organization reflects its orthodox Methodist origins. The largest administrative unit is the Episcopal District. Each Episcopal District is subdivided into Annual Conferences which in turn are composed of Presiding Elders Districts. Each Presiding Elder District is composed of a number of circuits or local congregations.

There are 18 Episcopal Districts in the A.M.E. church, 4 of which are in Africa. Zambia is in the seventeenth Episcopal District, along with Southern Rhodesia, Malawi, and several congregations in Zaire and Tanzania. In 1970, the church in Zambia was composed of 2 Annual Conferences, 12 Presiding Elders Districts, and 96 circuits.

Each of the structural units within the church has its corresponding head. The Episcopal Districts are supervised by bishops—

one for each Episcopal District—who have almost complete authority over its affairs. Bishops are elected by the General Conference in the United States every 4 years and remain bishops for life. Only in one instance has an African been elected to the rank of bishop and, in the seventeenth Episcopal District, the supervising bishop has always been an American.

As far as Zambia is concerned, however, the bishop has almost always governed *in absentia*. Until U.D.I. in Southern Rhodesia, American bishops to the seventeenth Episcopal District have resided in Bulawayo or have preferred to live in the United States and to administer the Episcopal District through an appointed deputy, referred to as the General Superintendent or Bishop's Agent. The post of bishop's deputy, thus, was the highest post to which a Zambian could, for all practical purposes, rise within the church. Because of the power of this position, it has been the focal point of political infighting and competition.

Annual Conferences have supervisors, usually referred to as vice-presidents. Like the bishop's deputy, they are appointed by the bishop and are sometimes used as vehicles to administer the Episcopal District in place of a bishop's deputy. As in the case of the Bishop's deputy, these posts assume considerable power given the usual absence of the bishop and are therefore coveted.

The positions of bishop's deputy and Annual Conference vice-president are posts which fall outside the standard A.M.E. hierarchy, having been created as a means of supervising Episcopal Districts in Africa. As a result, qualifications for the positions, terms of office, duties, responsibility, authorities, and the like, have not been promulgated and the choice of appointments is entirely at the bishop's discretion.

After the bishop, the post of Presiding Elder is the next highest position provided for in the normal A.M.E. hierarchy. Presiding Elders are ordained elders of the church, appointed annually by the bishops to supervise districts within the Annual Conferences. The bishop makes these appointments, however, in consultation with the other Presiding Elders. In fact, there is a Presiding Elders' Council which advises the bishop on most matters and which assumes increased power when the bishop is frequently absent. In 1968, there were 12 Presiding Elders and 44 ordinary elders in the Zambian church.

The leadership positions in the church are held by men, but the Women's Missionary Society is a major force in church affairs, particularly in the circuits. It is organized at the Episcopal District,

Annual Conference, Presiding Elders' District, and circuit levels. The bishop's wife is automatically the Episcopal Supervisor of the Women's Missionary Society in her husband's Episcopal District. The wife of the bishop's deputy is usually the President of the Women's Missionary Society in the Episcopal District. Similarly, the wife of the head of each unit in the church organization is almost always the leader of the women's organization in that unit. The other officers are elected, but the rank of one's husband does influence the voting.

The other major nonclerical group is the Laymen's Organization. It is also organized at the Episcopal District, Annual Conference, Presiding Elders' District, and circuit levels. But, unlike the Women's Missionary Society, it exerts most of its influence at the Episcopal District level. The lay leaders are often individuals who hold positions of authority, responsibility, and status within the community. They include chiefs, businessmen, civil servants, and other relatively successful and sophisticated members of the church. Indeed, as the influence of the Laymen's Organization is a function of the prestige and acumen of its members, frequently it is in a position to challenge the clergy on specific issues or for popular support from the membership. Hence they are a political force with which the clergy must always reckon.

Each of the subdivisions within the church and the major lay organizations have annual meetings at which appointments are made, major decisions taken, income and disbursements accounted for, and plans made for the coming year. Since the business has to do with power, money, and prestige, the meetings are political as well as organizational events. In addition, the social interaction also makes them major social occasions.

Like the larger church organization, the structure of the local circuits follows the established Methodist pattern. The head of the circuit is the pastor. According to the *A.M.E. Discipline,* one must have completed secondary school in order to be eligible to enter into the ministry. However, because of the scarcity of educational opportunities for Africans in colonial Northern Rhodesia, the effective rule became that a man must be literate in his own language.

Other leaders within the circuit include assistant pastors, underpastors, a chief steward, class leaders, deacons, and officials of the local Women's Missionary Society and Laymen's Organization. As in many other African churches, there is a proliferation of official positions. In one typical circuit, one person in every five could be said to be an official of that circuit (Johnson 1977:69).

The circuit is governed by an Official Board, composed of all officers of the circuit. Its weekly meetings are formal, with the pastor serving as chairman. The Official Board receives contributions from the membership, reports on various activities, hears disciplinary cases, and makes decisions regarding the management of the circuit. Within the formal structure, an informal leadership core often emerges as the effective governing unit.

In addition to the Sunday services, the activities of the circuit include meetings of the Women's Missionary Society and Laymen's Organization and various fund-raising projects. However, the most important activity is visiting. Officials of the circuit, especially the pastor, his wife, and the class leaders, are expected to pay regular visits to the membership. This pastoral care is also a major activity of the Women's Missionary Society and is the most important force that binds the circuit membership together.

The circuits in Zambia have always suffered from a lack of financial resources. Sunday collections provide some income, but the main source of revenue is the monthly dues of approximately 75 cents which each member is expected to pay. In almost every circuit, however, income is not adequate even to support the pastor fully, much less provide for growth and improvement of facilities. The circuits must therefore look to the Annual Conference for financial assistance of various kinds. Unfortunately, the Annual Conference receives most of its funds from the Presiding Elders' districts, which, in turn, depend upon poor circuits. Thus, the church in Zambia does not generate enough income to finance its own expansion and it must depend upon contributions from the church in America. Funds from the United States have not been forthcoming in large amounts and the scarce dollars which do come are controlled exclusively by the bishop.

The church has no distinctive doctrine or theology. Its belief system and ritual are orthodox and standard for the A.M.E. church everywhere. In bringing together various congregations from the Methodist Episcopal Church, the A.M.E. made no fundamental changes in its religious beliefs and ritual. In 1880, the church adopted the Methodist Book of Common Prayer in its entirety. The church in Zambia adheres strictly to the resulting doctrine and regulations which are codified in the *A.M.E. Discipline.*

The organization of the services, the music, the structure of the church government, and the nature of the prayer and worship show only few influences from indigenous culture. There are no special shrines or sacred objects and no spirit possession, drumming, or dancing during the services. There are no special commandments regarding prayers, giving alms, fasting, or preaching and no special prohibition on such things as sex or food.

III

Given the orthodoxy of its belief, ritual, and organization, how can one account for the emergence and early success of the A.M.E. church? One cannot maintain that the A.M.E. has a uniquely appropriate system of religious beliefs. Nor can it be argued that the church was constructed to suit African needs. Rather, it appears that the growth of the church during the 1930s, 1940s, and 1950s, and its demise during the 1960s must be related to its social role in Northern Rhodesian society. For many years the A.M.E. church had relatively distinctive attributes given the social context in which it operated. Hence its appeal and social significance during the early years. With the passsage of time, however, conditions changed. The church was no longer distinctive in its role; consequently a process of relative decline in appeal and social importance occurred.

There are two features of Northern Rhodesian society that were particularly relevant to our analysis. The first is that Northern Rhodesia was a plural society. The extent and nature of social differentiation based on race placed it near apartheid in terms of degree of pluralism. The second feature is that Northern Rhodesia was experiencing rapid social change—in particular, urbanization. During the period 1930–1960, Northern Rhodesia was transformed from an unindustrialized country with a mostly rural population to a relatively industrialized country with a large urban African population. There are several implications of these features for the A.M.E. church.

Northern Rhodesian society, through law and custom, was characterized by widespread segregation and discrimination against blacks. Africans were forced to carry passes, were segregated in public facilities, were not allowed equal access to education, and were prohibited from holding all but the lowest positions in employment.

From the point of view of attracting members, the plural character of the society gave the A.M.E. some relatively distinctive membership advantages. There were advantages for African clergy who belonged to the A.M.E. church. Of most importance, perhaps, was the fact that the A.M.E. ministers were ordained. For a man pursuing a career in the ministry, opportunities to become ordained are essential. With ordination come the rank, prestige, and authority that a successful minister must have. Between 1930 and the early 1960s, the A.M.E. church was one of the few denominations in which an African was likely to become ordained and where the ministry would have the long-term career prospects of a profession.

The church's appeal to the laity was primarily a result of two factors. First, there were clear emotional and psychological gratifications to be derived from membership in the A.M.E. church. And second, A.M.E. church membership furnished one of the few avenues open to the urban dweller for participation in organized civic activities.

On the first point, its history in the United States and South Africa helped establish the church's image of support for black causes because in those countries the very founding of the church was a protest against segregation and discrimination. In addition, in colonial Northern Rhodesia, the church consciously identified with the plight of the African masses. Representative of the church's position in this regard are the following statements made in the Northern Rhodesia Annual Conferences of 1953 and 1955. Referring to the "state of the country," the 1953 Conference said, in part, "Racial discrimination is robbing our country of the freedom enjoyed by other countries. So the church as a Christian organization should not keep quiet but join other denominations in denouncing these unchristian and discriminatory practices which are contrary to democratic principles and are debarring our nation from industrial, economic, and political development. . . ." Commenting in 1955 on the "state of the country," the conference concluded, "We need to remind ourselves that the A.M.E. Church is not a political body, yet as a church we should join in condemning injustice and oppression. We should be careful not to isolate ourselves from the masses in their cry and struggle for Christian justice and freedom. . . ."

For the African in Northern Rhodesia, the A.M.E. church also played an important psychological role. The A.M.E. church was an established, international Christian denomination with orthodox beliefs and rituals, and to many Northern Rhodesians, being modern meant being Christian. Yet it was also a black church, controlled by local people. By belonging to it, the Northern Rhodesian felt that he was affirming his African heritage rather than identifying with the social dominant whites by joining "their" church.

On the second point, the church offered large numbers of Northern Rhodesians the possibility of functioning in an organized civic group, of competing for prestige, of being elected to office, and of exercising power and authority within the local community. Significantly, the church became established before the welfare associations, trade unions, and political parties began to operate on a large scale. Therefore, at one point, church membership was the only form of organized civic activity for many urban Africans. And even after the emergence of the other organizations, churches remained the most broadly based because they were not limited to particular interest groups. The positions of class leader, steward, underpastor, deacon, and the like were roles that responded to the emerging system of norms and values. They reflected modern methods of exercising leadership, acquiring power and authority, and obtaining status and prestige. They permitted and encouraged the formation of social relationships based upon the requirements of urban life.

The plural character of Northern Rhodesia constituted the atmosphere in which African nationalism emerged. And even though it was not actively involved in the political struggle, the A.M.E. church did relate positively to the new black consciousness.

First, the entire leadership of this international church was black, including the bishops. The very existence of such an organization refuted the notion that blacks could not control their own affairs.

Second, the A.M.E. had an important image-making quality in that its membership included blacks of great stature. Among the accomplished American blacks who served in Southern Africa are H.M. Turner, L.J. Coppin, W.T. Vernon, and R.R. Wright. Among the historic figures from Southern Africa are John Dube, Hastings Banda, and Kenneth Kanunda. Not only were there great leaders who were associated with the church, but there was a broader base of African patriots in the church's membership. In Zambia, its membership included Justin Chimba, trade union leader and former cabinet minister; Robert Makasa, pioneer political activist and government minister; W.K. Sikalumbi, political organizer and Member of Parliament; Issac Mumpansha, welfare leader and former Ambassador to Germany; J.M.B. Siyomunji, cabinet minister; Titus Mukupo, political journalist; Hosea Soko, former Ambassador to the United States and to the Soviet Union; A.J. Soko, cabinet minister; and H.B. Kalanga, leading political organizer prior to independence.

It should be clearly understood that the A.M.E. church did not participate in political activity. No A.M.E. ministers have led political movements, for instance, and the church was seldom associated with "political" events. It was the intrinsic nature and character of the church within the particular sociopolitical context of colonial Northern Rhodesia that differentiated it from most other religious denominations. As evidence of this point, one could cite the A.M.E. local preacher who, in 1937, asked of a district officer, without provocation, "Why do you divide out the land? I am an African. The land belongs to us Africans. We don't come from overseas [Johnson 1977: 31]."

Notwithstanding its support for African nationalism, the most significant attribute of the A.M.E. church was its relationship to the social change that was taking place. We know that social change involves the acquisition of new patterns of social organization and new norms and values (Epstein 1958; Mitchell 1954). In Northern Rhodesia there were material and other advantages to individuals who learned the roles and who acquired the values and norms of the achievement-oriented society. Particularly among the emerging elite in the urban areas, new patterns of social organization were adopted, and institutions that could embody, transmit, and employ these patterns were required.

Which institutions would fulfill this function? Traditional institutions were not appropriate and, in the segregated society, white institutions could not be used. One would expect the African community to establish its own new institutions under such circumstances. This it did. The A.M.E. church was one such institution.

The very organization of the church is significant in this context because it was thoroughly Western. It was an international organization, with a multinational and multiethnic membership and clergy. The leaders—pastors, stewards, class leaders, presiding elders, church secretaries, and the like—performed modern roles and were evaluated in terms of modern norms. The management of the church involved meetings patterned on Robert's Rules of Order, the use of western financial and record-keeping procedures, conducting community groups such as the Women's Missionary Society and Laymen's Organization, and so on. All of this, of course, both reflected and promoted a new set of values within the urban African community and occurred during the period when few other institutions stood in this relationship to social change.

To demonstrate in greater detail how the A.M.E. church functioned as an instrument of social change, the role of the church as an adaptive institution can be cited. In the first instance, the nature of the church's relationship to traditional culture facilitated the continuation of relevant traditional norms and thus aided adjustment to changing circumstances. Second, the A.M.E. circuit assisted adjustment to change by performing many of the functions of a voluntary association.

On the first point, the customs associated with death provide an example of traditional norms and values that have been continued in the functioning of the church. The nature of visiting obligations in circumstances of death reflect traditional attitudes of propriety. Mourners are expected to gather at the house of the deceased, where they quietly, chat, or drink beer. At about sundown, drums begin to beat, singing and weeping begins, and individuals extol the virtues of the deceased person. The singing, drumming, weeping, and exhortation continues until about midnight, when everyone goes to sleep. Shortly before daybreak, the weeping, singing, and drumming begins again. This pattern is repeated for several days.

During the actual funeral services, the wife of the deceased sits to the right side of the casket, weeping and wailing. Friends sit near her and comfort her, but they weep as well. At the end of the service, while the casket is being taken from the church, the weeping and wailing increase. The depth of feeling is so great that usually some of the women must be physically aided.

The pertinent sociological point is that being present at the long period of mourning, publicly extolling the deceased's virtues, and manifesting extreme grief are sometimes socially required in situations of death. Traditionally, these practices strengthened social bonds, provided assistance to the family of the deceased, and avoided allegations of witchcraft. A modern institution that accommodates this social reality and that allows the continuation of appropriate forms of behavior clearly eases the stresses of social change for the individuals involved.

The perpetuation of traditional culture elements is also seen in the interpretation of misfortune—particularly in the continuance of witchcraft beliefs. Officially, the A.M.E. church does not believe in witchcraft. There is no mechanism to combat witchcraft and the church takes the same public position as the white churches regarding witchcraft. At the same time, though, the belief in witches is not actively campaigned against and it does remain part of the belief system with which the members deal with life's problems. Members use African doctors freely. Indeed, even A.M.E. ministers often consult herbalists and African doctors.

Witchcraft beliefs have been shown to respond to the individual's psychological needs and to help maintain the social order (Mayer 1954; Marwick 1952; Evans-Pritchard 1937). In this regard, we must remind ourselves that in social change the individual does not suddenly discard "old" patterns of social organization in favor of the "new" ones. Rather, the "old" and "new" systems of social relationships exist simultaneously and one must exercise "situational selection" in determining appropriate norms for a given situation (Mitchell 1969). Thus, given their social and instrumental function, the need for witchcraft beliefs persists among urban dwellers.

The theoretical point is that the A.M.E. church facilitated the use of social relationships and customs from traditional society at times when alternative norms were unavailable or unacceptable. Particularly in times of crisis, it permitted traditional methods of coping to persist.

Also increasing its effectiveness with regard to social change was the way the church functioned as a voluntary association. It offered its members a sense of belonging·in an urban environment where kinship did not provide automatic membership in a support group. It offered aid in a situation where impersonal social relationships made no provision for aid. It offered recreation in circumstances where one had to establish relationships based upon nontraditional criteria. And it provided an agent of social control in an atmosphere of changing norms.

The sense of belonging was accomplished by the issuance of membership cards, by reserving special privileges for members, and by allowing individuals to have membership rights in A.M.E. congregations elsewhere in the country. The mutual aid was institutionalized in the norms of membership and was executed, in large part, in the "pastoral care" and "visitation" conducted by the circuit. The extensive visiting was also a principal source of entertainment, although recreation sometimes took the form of secular functions or elements of fun, such as competitions, introduced into regular church activities. The social control function of the circuit was exercised through the judicial and decision-making role it played in the nonreligious lives of the membership. The great asset of the church in performing this function was its ability to operate within the value system of members, which incorporated traditional as well as modern norms.

IV

Unlike the situation in some parts of West Africa and southern Africa, there has not been a proliferation of African Christian movements in Zambia. The short-lived Church of Zion appeared in Lusaka in 1922 and, about 1925, Tomo Nyirenda declared himself Mwana Lesa (The Son of God) and proceeded to kill 200 "witches." There have been, however, two major African Christian movements in

Zambia—the Watchtower Movement (the Jehovah's Witnesses) and the Lumpa Church. A brief comparison of these movements with the A.M.E. church will place the preceding analysis in clearer focus.

Having been established shortly after World War I, the Watchtower developed a large following during the 1920s. It was similar to the A.M.E. church in that it originated in the United States, it was largely administered by local people, and it had the "feel" of an African church. The political and social conditions described in relation to the A.M.E. church were factors influencing the growth of the Watchtower Movement as well.

Unfortunately, the descriptions of the Watchtower do not provide detailed information on the organization and functioning of the Watchtower church, so comparison with the A.M.E. in this regard is difficult (Assimeng 1970; Meebelo 1971). Other important points do emerge from the literature however.

The first significant fact is that the Watchtower was predominately a rural movement. It catered to a peasant class which, although experiencing social change, was not in the same social situtation as the middle classes in the towns. Changes in role relationships and adaption to different norms and values proceeded at a much slower pace in the rural areas. Moreover, the shifts in patterns of social organization in the rural areas were not as severe, and thus there was less need for institutions to ease the tension of change.

The second point which the literature makes is that the Watchtower doctrine rejected involvement in the wider world. Assimeng (1970:107) notes that, ". . . its value system is at variance with that of the society in which it operates." In other words, Watchtower was not an agent of modernization. Its focus on witch-hunting and the millenium was meaningful to some people in the rural areas, but it was largely irrelevant to the emerging elites in the towns. The townsman required a world view which helped him integrate into urban life, not a doctrine which alienated him from it.

The Lumpa movement dates its beginning to the mid—1950s when Alice Lenshina first had her vision. In contrasting the Lumpa church with the A.M.E. church, though, basically the same points can be made as were made with regard to the Watchtower. Again, the literature provides little analysis of the administrative structure and daily functioning of the church, except to say that the organization was not sufficiently complex for the large number of adherents (Roberts 1970; Rotberg 1961). But like the Watchtower, the Lumpa church was a rural movement whose doctrine was otherworldly and opposed to all secular authority. It was also primarily concerned with combating witchcraft. Hence, the Lumpa church had only an indirect relationship to the pluralism and urbanization which were dominant features in the towns.

Although both the Watchtower and Lumpa movements were larger than the A.M.E. church, their relative absence from urban centers seems to confirm the distinctive role and function of the A.M.E. church as a social institution. It was organized along Western lines, was concerned about modernizing forces such as African education, and supported African nationalism. One can understand why the A.M.E. church rather than Watchtower or Lumpa, was the church of much of the African elite. Its task was to be integrated into the new social system, to adopt the values and norms required for success, and to exercise authority in terms of the "new" legitimation.

The church's demise and the failure of the present Zambian elite to belong to it, can also be explained in terms of pluralism and continuing social change. In the highly plural colonial society, the sharp cleavage between white and black were the only distinctions which could be called "class" divisions. Although there was a group of urban, educated Africans who have been referred to as the African "middle class" or the African "elite," sociologically this group did not constitute a social class. The racial cleavages were so sharp that they tended to minimize the differences within the African population.

With independence and the lessening of pluralism, there has been a tendency for factors of class to become more consequential. The new "elite" has adopted a life-style that is drastically different from their old one and from the life-style of most A.M.E. members. Most have traveled abroad, now live in houses formerly reserved for whites, drive large automobiles, and frequent expensive places of entertainment. The important issues in their lives are issues which are important nationally and internationally.

It is not suggested that "social classes" have actually emerged in Zambia. There are, for example, strong ties of kinship which cut across and weaken the bonds of social class. Rather, it is only suggested that the factors tending toward the proliferation of social classes are more in evidence now than during the intense pluralism of the colonial period and that these factors are, in part, responsible for the widening of the gap between the interests of the A.M.E. members and the nation's leaders.

Thus it was the plural character of the colonial society and the process of urbanization that gave the A.M.E. church a distinctive social role and importance. As the society has become more heterogeneous, other institutions have become responsive to African needs. Furthermore, the process of institutionalizing new forms of social organization and new norms has now proceeded to the point that the stresses of social change have been reduced. In the present social environment, the A.M.E. church has no socially significant role to play —hence, it is on the decline.

REFERENCES

Assimeng, J.M. 1970 "Sectarian Allegiance and Political Aurthority: The Watchtower Society in Zambia, 1907-35," *Journal of Modern African Studies,* I, 8.

Coan, J. 1961 *Expansion of Missions of the African Methodist Episcopal Church in South Africa, 1896-1908.* Hartford, Conn.: Hartford Seminary Ph.D. Dissertation.

DuBois, W.E.B. 1899 *The Philadelphia Negro.* New York: Benjamin Blom, Inc.

Epstein, A.L. 1958 *Politics in an Urban African Community.* Manchester: Manchester University Press.

Evans-Pritchard, E.E. 1937 *Witchcraft, Oracles, and Magic Among the Azande.* Oxford: Clarendon Press.

Favre, E. 1913 *François Coillard: Missionaire au Zambèze 1882–1904.* Paris: Société de Missions Évangelizues.

Flournoy, B.M. 1976 "The Relationship of the African Methodist Episcopal Church to its South African Members, 1896-1906," *Journal of African Studies,* II, 4.

Hall, R. 1965 *Zambia.* London: Pall Mall Press.

Johnson, W.R. 1977 *Worship and Freedom: A Black American Church in Zambia.* London: International African Institute.

———— 1978 "The A.M.E. Church and Ethiopianism in South Africa," *Journal of Southern African Affairs,* III, No. 2.

Marwick, M.G. 1952 "The Social Context of Cewa Witch Beliefs," *Africa,* 22.

Mayer, P. 1954 *Witches.* Grahamstown: Rhodes University Press.

Meebelo, H.S. 1971 *Reaction to Colonialism.* Manchester: Institute for African Studies.

Mitchell, J.C. 1954 "African Urbanization in Ndola and Luanshya," *Rhodes-Livingstone Communication,* 6.

———— 1969 (ed.) *Social Networks in Urban Situations.* Manchester: Manchester University Press.

Ranger, T.O. 1965 "The Ethiopian Episode in Barotseland, 1900-1905," *Rhodes-Livingstone Journal,* 37.

Roberts, A.D. 1970 "The Lumpa Church of Alice Lenshina," in Rotberg, R. and Mazrui, A. *Protest and Power in Black Africa,* New York: Oxford University Press.

Rotberg, R. 1961 "The Lenshina Movement of Northern Rhodesia," *Rhodes-Livingstone Journal,* 29.

Roux, E. 1964 *Time Longer than Rope.* Madison: University of Wisconsin Press.

Singleton, G.A. 1952 *The Romance of African Methodism.* New York: Exposition Press.

IV

Bennetta Jules-Rosette

PROPHECY AND LEADERSHIP IN THE MARANKE CHURCH
A Case Study in Continuity and Change

Outside observers often characterize African churches as schismatic; however, the details of these conflicts are seldom analyzed. The fissive tendencies of these churches must be seen in terms of the overall expansion of each group. This discussion will analyze the organization of an indigenous African church outside of mission aegis and the relationship between schism and centralization within it. The Apostolic Church of John Maranke (Vapostori) was founded in Zimbabwe, then Southern Rhodesia, in 1932 during a period of rising religious activity among various Shona groups. The Maranke church gradually spread from Umtali northward to Salisbury and then beyond the borders of Zimbabwe as far north as what is now the Republic of Zaire.

As a child, John Maranke, a muShona whose father married into the family of chief Maranke, is said to have experienced extraordinary visions. He asserted that his calling was confirmed in childhood by Methodist missionaries who viewed the recurrent illness of their pupil as a form of spiritual inspiration. In July of 1932, 10 years after his initial inspiration, John recruited the first church members

109

AFRICAN CHRISTIANITY
Patterns of Religious Continuity

from his extended family. By baptizing his older brothers and a maternal cousin, he established the church's leadership base. Others within the Maranke reserve and beyond flocked to the new church for faith healing and the promise of miracles to be wrought. That July, John baptized an estimated 150 converts en masse in "the Jordan," actually the Murozvi river that crosses the Maranke Reserve (Daneel 1971:323). The congregation went on to become one of the major Central and Southern African indigenous churches during the late colonial period.

Forty-two years after the first baptismal and Sabbath celebrations, the Maranke Apostles have spread across six Central African countries with an estimated membership of more than 500,000 persons.[1] No longer does the small Zimbabwean leadership cadre provide the sole political direction for the church. Its regional members, although confirmed and reviewed by the central leadership, operate autonomously in their congregations. Outlying Zimbabwean congregations can readily consult the core hierarchy concerning doctrine and ritual. Many of them share a Shona ethnic and social background. However, in congregations outside of Zimbabwe, a multiplicity of interpretations of belief and practice have arisen. These interpretations were adapted to local custom and circumstances and often required considerable modification of the original church practices accepted in the founding branch. To understand the present organization of the Apostolic Church, it is, therefore, necessary to examine leadership innovations in the context of the church's international growth.

THE HISTORICAL CONTEXT OF CHURCH EXPANSION

The Maranke church is characterized by two distinct forms of missionizing. In the first, which may be termed "missionizing in reverse," Apostles from outlying congregations visited the centers of religious learning and returned with newly acquired convictions and practices to proselytize in their home areas (cf. Barrett 1968: 73–75,

---

1. Barret (1968:296) estimated a total of 50,000 Maranke Apostles in Zimbabwe and 40,000 members in the Zaire. His estimates were based on paschal attendance and statements from individual congregations in 1964 and 1965. He did not have estimates for Malawi, Mozambique, Angola, Zambia, or South Africa. Barrett considered his estimates to be underrepresentations of the growing Maranke population (personal communication, 1972).

173). In the second, termed *matimana* (teaching journey) by Apostles, representatives from the church's headquarters or other established congregations traveled long distances to evangelize in new areas or to provide both encouragement and an organizational check on newer branches. The first pattern became the predominant mode through which official leadership hierarchies were established in the new congregations. The core of this hierarchy, following a pattern originated by John Maranke in about 1940, consisted of a committee of 12 high officers approved of by the founding prophet. Each officer had one of four spiritual gifts: baptism, preaching, prophecy, or healing, at one of three organizational grades. Those holding the highest grade of "Lieb-Umah" (community leader) were considered to be "high priests," responsible politically only to "the messenger," John Maranke, and otherwise autonomous.

The early Maranke Apostles formed missionary cadres that left Umtali, going as far north as the Copperbelt.[2] Many of these members settled in Zambia, where they formed the core membership. However, the establishment of formal outlying congregations, recognized as politically distinct and yet articulated with the central leadership, awaited the process of sending new members who claimed to have experienced miraculous cures and conversions back to their own families and homelands.[3] Later in the church's development, the *matimana* or formal 2-year mission journey was established as a way in which young members could dedicate themselves to the church and its teachings. Nevertheless, the predominant means of building new congregations in outlying areas remained the pattern of "missionizing in reverse," in which local residents traveled to the church center of their own accord and then proselytized among their own groups. Soon, the combined impact of these strategies resulted in a church that transcended tribal, ethnic, and cultural boundaries.

By the 1940s, Apostles had established *kereks* (congregations) in Zambia, and within 10 years reverse missionaries were also returning from Zaire. Although the group's spiritual appeal was still based on claims of miraculous healing and prophecy, its audience had shifted. The earlier Zimbabwean members had been rural. The mushrooming founding community lived, farmed, and worshiped on the

2. Tshibangu (1970:4) and personal communications from Maranke informants indicate that Shona-speaking Apostles traveled as far north as Lusaka in search of new converts as early as 1948.

3. Maranke (1953:23–25). Early converts came to the Maranke Reserve from Salisbury in search of cure. When they were healed, they returned to the city with news of John and his Apostles.

Maranke Reserve. Many of the new converts from Salisbury and the outlying congregations were different. They journeyed to Maranke for instruction and cure, and they regarded the church center as a "hospital" for the chronically ill. They lived on a transitory basis in urban centers and found in the church a way of preserving home ties and a concern for ceremony. While both rural and urban Apostles may be viewed as somewhat "encapsulated," the urban members found in Apostlehood a new identity and a supporting network in town.[4] They were able to remain in urban areas and participate in a cash economy without accepting a way of life alien to them. It is from this kernel of itinerant merchants, miners, railroad workers, and "jacks of all trades" located in and around the urban centers that the Zairean congregations began to grow.

Members from all congregations maintained an overriding interest in the annual Passover ceremony, which established central organizational control and a point of personal contact with the founder. The Passover was a unique attempt to solve the problems of reconciling prophecy and leadership over a rapidly expanding organization. Beginning with the original Passover site on the Maranke Reserve John traveled annually to a growing number of Passover locations, where he instituted committees of 12, over which he retained the ultimate political control.

As the Maranke church spread away from its original centers in the 1940s and 1950s, it became more difficult for the Zimbabwean hierarchy to monitor innovations in beliefs and ritual practices. Local leaders attempted to bring John to their home congregations to celebrate the Passover, to confirm their own leadership positions, to legitimate their authority, and to provide charismatic encouragement for their followers. Whether or not a local Passover jurisdiction was formed, these leaders were considered responsible to the Zimbabwean church headquarters, both spiritually and politically. They, however, did not always have access to religious rulings concerning the separation of ceremonial activities, the use of liturgy, and the relevance of local traditional religions for Apostles. The local leaders did not maintain close contact in many cases, but traveled periodically to visit the Zimababwean elders at the main Passover ceremony, where they renewed organizational ties and raised questions of political import for their home congregations.

The growing contrast between congregational leaders who re-

4. Mayer (1961:90) describes encapsulation as the process by which urban migrants maintain unbroken contact with their country home and abstain from unnecessary contact with activities outside the group.

peatedly made the pilgrimage to the church's center at Bocha village on the Maranke reserve in Eastern Zimbabwe and the majority of members of their congregations who could not afford the trip, strengthened the role of local leaders as intermediaries between their groups and the central hierarchy. Gradually, a tension developed between the ideal of visionary inspiration for all Apostles and the actual political complications accompanying an international organization based on the committees of 12 and attendance at the Zimbabwean Passover. This tension increasingly became focused in power struggles between individual leaders competing for the role of intermediary with the center. Apostolic political decisions were cross-checked by visionary expressions regardless of the status and activities of the individuals involved. The present organizational pressures have resulted in a major schism extending across a number of congregations. This schism has not undercut the church's international base, but it has made the status of several elders in outlying congregations problematic, both as Apostles and as members of the founding church. These recent political developments will be discussed in more detail in the following sections.

To provide the historical and organizational background for these developments, I shall describe the process through which the church was established in the Zaire in the 1950s and the organizational results of geographic diffusion. I shall then return to the succession crisis in the central Zimbabwean church that followed the death of the founding prophet in 1963 and its effects on the treatment of outlying congregations. With this background, the power struggle that arose and that has persisted in the Zairean church, can be placed in its full historical perspective.

APOSTLES OF THE ZAIRE: A FOREIGN CHURCH IN A FOREIGN LAND

Apostles have written and told the stories of their expansion in the form of intricate myths that treat each event as sacred. This history is particularly important to the Apostles of the Zaire, for it links their church spiritually to its Zimbabwean foundation. Nawezi Petro, the first Lunda member and the first Zairean convert, is said to have entered Zambia with his wife Tshibola Marie, in March of 1953.[5]

---

5. Tshibangu (1970:2-4) describes Marie's illness, search for cure, and baptism. He gives a detailed description of Nawezi's original Apostolic commission.

Suffering from tuberculosis, she had come to the Apostles in a des-
perate search for cure. Their "prophets" took her to a secluded area
near Lusaka and promised that cure would follow her baptism. After
a dramatic night ceremony in which a paralytic was healed, Marie
was baptized the following morning and was reported to have
vomited out the evil spirits causing her illness. Nawezi's baptism followed immediately upon this miraculous proof of cure. He became
the first member to cross the border into the Zaire with the news of
the Apostles and their message of spiritual healing.

According to John's instructions, Nawezi attempted to convert
members of his own family but was largely unsuccessful. Nevertheless, several of his wife's relatives, BaLuba from the Kasai area, eventually joined. After a year of preaching, Nawezi had only seven members. Young Musumbu Pierre, of Luba extraction and a relative of
Tshibola Marie, joined. Musumbu later began to experience extraordinary visions that attracted many new converts, particularly
Kasians. The boldness and accuracy of Musumbu's visions gave him a
charismatic appeal that extended across several congregations.

Nawezi's daughter was proclaimed a prophetess by the church
elders, but her participation in the group was sporadic. By 1971,
when I first interviewed Nawezi, she was no longer a member of the
Lubumbashi congregation. Even though membership gradually grew,
Nawezi felt the continual pressures of external political attacks. In
November 1956, the Maranke church was formally outlawed in the
Shaba province by a ruling based on 1926 ordinance forbidding "indigenous assocations whose existence could counteract the civiliza-
tion of the natives or constitute a menace to tranquility and public
order."[6] An article in the provincial press, favoring interdiction,
compared the church with the Kimbanguist and Kitawala movements, which it described as regressive politico-religious sects led by
false prophets who "promised the moon to their followers."[7] It
further declared that the movement was subversive and played on the
credulity of the population. In the face of this opposition, Nawezi
continued to petition the colonial authorities for recognition and was
arrested 16 times in connection with church activities between 1956
and 1966.

By 1956, the church had spread to the West Kasai through the

6. This information is contained in the records of the Belgian territorial administrators
(Moriame 1956; Rutten 1926). The information was released to the churches after Independence.

7. This article appeard in late 1956 in a Lubumbashi newspaper, "Interdiction d'une
secte indigene au Katanga," Essor du Congo, November 12, 1956.

efforts of an anonymous woman and Mujanaie Marcel, an itinerant Kasaian laborer who had journeyed to Shaba and Zambia in search of employment in the copper mines.[8] It is unclear from the Apostles' accounts whether Mujanaie had much direct contact with Nawezi. Mujanaie joined with Kasanda Vincent, a self-styled visionary leader before his conversion to the apostolate, and Kadima Alphonse in a zealous campaign to gain converts in the Kasai area and in the towns and compounds along the rail lines between Lubumbashi and Kananga in southwestern Zaire. Mujanaie, who has since abandoned the church, wished to become the church's official leader in the two Kasai provinces. He vied with Kasanda for this position. Spurred by the restrictions placed on the Maranke Apostles in Shaba, colonial officials in the Kasai saw the possibility of weakening the group by creating further conflicts between Kasanda and Mujanaie (Goffard 1958).

The issue of health regulations became the focus of administrative discontent. Authorities insisted that Apostles comply with vaccination programs and blood tests, which were formally prohibited by the church's central hierarchy. Both Kasanda and Mujanaie were interrogated concerning the church's refusal to meet these demands. Kasanda replied with biblical citations supporting the strict use of faith healing (Hentgen 1958). He and Mujanaie requested time to consult with the church's central leadership. It was, however, not established who was to be the principal intermediary between the church and the authorities. As a result, the administration staged interviews to stimulate further conflict between the two (Hentgen 1958). Both leaders made pilgrimages to church headquarters at Bocha village on the Maranke reserve, but neither trusted the details of the other's report. After his final visit to Zimbabwe during the negotiations, Kasanda reiterated his original refusal to observe health measures but did not implement it as a church policy. Since no new incidents of resistance arose, the authorities allowed the medical impasse to drop (Hentgen 1959).

Within a few years, Mujanaie's challenge to leadership disappeared in the West Kasai. At this time, Kasanda headed the Kananga congregation which grew to at least 300 members, according to his rough estimation. He continued his journeys to Bocha to participate in the annual Passover ceremony and was confirmed first as a prophet

---

8. Mujanaie came to the attention of the colonial authorities when Apostles opposed them on health measures. Colonial documents indicate that this confrontation was underway by early 1958 (Lemborelle 1958).

by virtue of his visionary experience and much later as a congregational leader, or baptist Lieb-Umah, for Kananga.[9]

In 1959, Kasanda wrote a series of letters requesting the colonial government's permission to hold a Passover celebration in the
Kasai (Kasanda 1959). The request was refused on a technicality of
application procedure. Nevertheless, Kasanda repeated the request
every year from 1959 to 1963, when it was finally authorized by the
newly independent Republic of the Congo. The local Apostolic leaders were anxious for the Passover ceremony to take place so that spiritual offices could be confirmed for them and the four spiritual gifts
confirmed for the majority of their members. Although John Maranke had begun performing the ceremony in 1934 (Daneel 1971;
239), he did not leave Zimbabwe for the outlying congregations until
the late 1950s (Maranke 1953:21). In 1963, he did travel to Zaire
where he administered the Passover in several locations. Kasanda's
original request, however, was a rapid response to challenges about
the church's international mandate made by the central leadership at
Bocha.

The internal organization of the Zairean church emerges more
distinctly against the background of the Passover ceremony. Through
the Passover, John attempted to sustain the direct contact characteristic of a much smaller community within a rapidly expanding
church. Under the original plan, every member who partook of the
sacrament would meet John personally. The founder would also be
able to control individual adherence to ritual and doctrine by the
testimonies of prophets given at the Passover.

Unfavorable testimonies could lead to suspension or expulsion
from the church upon review by the committee of judges (*vatongi*) in
Bocha. The rapid increase of foreign congregations led John to enlist
the aid of his sons in traveling to outlying areas. In 1957, he sent his

9. There are four spiritual gifts for which members may be confirmed in the Apostolic Church: baptists or pastors, who begin and end the worship ceremony and baptize new
converts; evangelists or preachers, who organize the worship service and are most active in
preaching; healers, who pray for the sick; and prophets, who examine other members before
worship and give visionary communications. Women may be healers and prophets but not
baptists and evangelists. Men may hold any of the four gifts. The gifts are confirmed annually at the Passover ceremony along with organizational grades including the Lieb-Umah position. Murphree describes the importance of the Lieb-Umah (who may hold any of the four
gifts) at the Passover (1969: 99-100). Murphree (1969:99) and Heimer (1971:245) specu-
late about the etymological origins of the term. They both indicate the Hebrew *rabba,* great
or leader, and *ummah,* people or community, as origins. The Arabic *ummat,* or congregation, may also have inspired the word. However, Apostles claim that John received the term
in a vision and that it is purely of divine origin. For further distinctions among ranks, see
Jules-Rosette (1975:155-183).

eldest son, Abel Sithole, to the eastern districts of Zambia and to Mozambique and his second son, Makebi Sithole, to the western and southern portions of Zimbabwe. In this way, either John or his sons would confirm leaders in local congregations and judge personal and church disputes. His assistants would instruct the members in these areas in the songs and ceremonies of the church center.

Despite the paschal tour, further problems and readjustments faced the outlying churches. Local languages, customs, and taboos had to be integrated with the precedents set at Bocha. Often, it was difficult to separate Shona traditions from John's inspired reading of sacred texts and his interpretations of visionary experiences.[10] The dietary laws of the Old Testament were adapted to local foods and customs. The Apostles' revisions of various dowry systems and clanic marriage preferences were combined and adjusted within each region, although Apostolic endogamy was the guiding principle for all of the congregations. At the Passover ceremony, a new crop of eligible young women was scrutinized and presented to the elders each year in a revitalization of traditional marriage practice (Jules-Rosette 1976). Similarly, older practices of ancestor worship, while formally abandoned by the church, were integrated into the process of selecting a successor after John's death.[11]

Perhaps most apparent of all the modifications in the expanding church was the multiple language base that developed as Apostolic ceremonies spread outside of Zimbabwe. Although Chishona, actually a standardization of several local dialects, was used as a liturgical language in the four Apostolic hymns constituting the church's basic worship format, the distinctive vernacular versions of the Shona songs and new ones locally composed were introduced in the outlying congregations. Innovations were also made in the closely timed and formal oratorical style that had developed on the Maranke reserve. The rhythmic flow of preaching and Bible reading was broken by multilanguage recitations and the occasional addition of sermon translations. The overall effect was the creation of a ceremony conducted in songs and texts from diverse languages but adhering to the basic ritual format established in Zimbabwe. There emerged a ritual pattern in which the main features were recognizable to all members but in which ceremonial particulars differed from group to group.

10. A more comprehensive analysis of the mixture of spiritual inspiration, biblical exegesis, and traditional lore contained in Apostolic belief and practices appears in Jules-Rosette (1975).

11. Daneel (1971:333–335). Some members, however, particularly members of the church outside of Zimbabwe, deny the applicability of the term *kugadzira* to this ceremony.

The standard format of worship and the division of members into the four spiritual gifts allowed Apostles from all regions to grasp the content, social organization, and direction of a ceremony in spite of regional diversity. Ceremony, therefore, reinforced the possibility for plural, panethnic religious participation. The interactional differences in ceremony also represented political distinctions in the responsibilities of the members. The importance of an evangelist or preacher, who in some cases would have to master as many as five or six languages, was crucial in coordinating transitions from one speaker or Bible reader to the next during the main worship ceremony.

Possibilities for confusion and delay within a given ceremony were based on political as well as linguistic differences. Introducing a new language carried with it the challenge of its users as a subgroup within the congregation. Their relationships to other members would have to be assessed. In congregations where multiple language coordination was particularly important, the managing evangelist surpassed the pastor or baptist in actual authority and vied with him for special status.[12] The importance of managing multilingual ceremonies in which participants represented different subgroups in the international church sustained a built-in conflict or, at the very least, an ambiguity in the relationship between the head baptist and the managing evangelist of each congregation.

Despite its mandate to do so, the church center was not able to monitor the subtleties of congregational variations in worship. When disputes could not readily be resolved, the local groups were torn apart by schism. Difficulties in celebrating the Passover annually left large gaps in congregations, particularly those of the East and West Kasai provinces in the Zaire. There, the lack of internal contact among the Kasai and Shaba congregations increased the occasions for both division and diversity. Ethnic and political cleavages formed a constant backdrop for the baptist Nawezi's Lubumbashi congregation. When the prophet Musumbu gained a large following, his supporters formed their own congregation in the same town. The evangelist Kadima Alphonse, who at first joined Musumbu, later formed his own congregation. The schism extended beyond the Shaba province. Many Kasaian and some Zambian members followed Musumbu, and tales of his prophetic and leadership skills spread to their homelands. Others who did not know him often invoked their knowledge of the existing schisms in other areas as grounds for separate leadership challenge within their own congregations.

12. Case studies of multilingual performance in Sabbath ceremonies are presented in Jules-Rosette (1975) and Jules-Rosette (1977:185-216).

Detailed news of the outlying congregations reached Bocha only by those messengers who were able to make the journey. Reports were fragmentary and sporadic. Thus, in spite of John's direct control of congregations, his actual authority over the activities of their members expectably diminished as the outlying branches mushroomed. Regional centralization was also difficult. By the mid-1950s Nawezi's position as a "national" founder and as a regional leader was severely contested. In 1958, Nawezi was confirmed by John as a Lieb-Umah or congregational leader at a Passover held in Zambia. Even though Nawezi obtained this rank, his position was challenged by the schismatic local congregations. In 1961 Musumbu was confirmed as a second Lieb-Umah for the Lubumbashi area, and the church center simultaneously tried to reconcile the two rival factions by giving their leaders independent jurisdicitions.

CENTRALIZATION AND DIFFUSION

While each Maranke Apostle acknowledges John as the founder and all are considered equal in their spiritual mission, considerable ritual and political variation exists in the church. Despite ritual standards, even the basic format of prayer and ceromony differs from one region to another.[13] Marshall Murphree has referred to the Apostolic toleration for innovations in worship and doctrinal interpretations as "heterodoxy and heteropraxy."[14] He cites two basic

13. For example, while all Apostles face East when they pray, Apostles in Zambia temporarily innovated on the basic pattern. Under the original system, the rows of men are to the east of those of women, i.e., the men are in front of the women while praying. In Zambia, the rows were turned to the north and south of each other so that they were beside each other while praying. A Zambian prophet introduced this innovation, stating that God wants men and women to enter heaven as equals. However, the innovation was discarded a year later when visiting elders complained, and the central court at Bocha ruled it out of order.

14. Murphree (1969:165) states:

> Two types of mobility have been defined, affiliational mobility, in which an individual in the course of his lifetime changes his religious group membership one or more times; and temporary mobility, where an individual moves out of the pattern of belief and practices standard for his group and temporarily, for specific purposes, aligns himself with those of another. Among reasons for the first type of mobility are personality conflicts and role rivalries, factors often related to religious schism. But the second type is perhaps more important in this context. The acceptance by Vapostori of temporary mobility on the part of their members permits divergence from the norms of the group, while the privilege of membership is retained. Heterodoxy and heteropraxy do not

reasons for a heterodox orientation in the group: personality conflicts or rivalries and temporary individual mobility within and outside of the group. Whereas the first factor is certainly at the source
of religious schism, the second is regarded as an aspect of the Apostles' permissiveness in allowing their children to suspend religious
participation while attending mission schools or to compromise by
seeking traditional or modern medical care. None of these forms of
personal or social heterodoxy reflect, however, the difficulties that
arise in a large-scale church rather than a single congregation. They
do not indicate the conditions under which regional and social innovations become the Zimbabwean center's focus for scrutiny and
group exclusion.

It is tempting to regard the practices and growth of the sect in a
single area as representative of all of its congregations. However, it
has already been noted that the process of dispersion in the Apostolic case created distinctions between urban and rural subgroups,
between ethnically diverse and ethnically homogeneous congregations. Political centralization relied heavily on regular celebration of
the Passover, often impossible in the more remote areas. Ceremonial
continuity was based on oral teaching and the gradual transmission
of ritual practices from one area to another. If the "missionaries in
reverse" failed to grasp their instructions fully or if they received the
teachings in areas far from Bocha, drastic discrepancies in ritual practices occurred. One informant reported, with profound disapproval,
a congregation in which women carried the long staffs reserved for
Apostolic men and wore the men's ritual undergarments. Such puta-
tive deviations would have been censored if the news of their existence had reached the church's center.

Thus, diversified "foreign" congregations magnified the problems of heterodoxy and removed them from the scale of individual
transgressions. Every sect beyond Bocha, and particularly the non-
Zimbabwean congregations, collectively faced the possibility that its
entire membership might be ruled "out of order" or "in a state of
sin" by the central judges and Zimbabwean committee of twelve.[15]
If an entire congregation had not celebrated the Passover in several
years, it was, according to John's own pronouncements, slipping
further and further away from the hope of salvation. It risked being
riddled with disputes and divided by schism. Its ritual innovations,

---

therefore necessarily lead to expulsion, nor to the formation of groups of mal-
contents seeking to create new groups with revised standards.

15. Court cases are judged in Zimbabwe by a *dare* or open court consisting of special
evangelists. Local cases are also heard by evangelist-judges for each region.

including songs and sermons of a partisan nature, would have been allowed to grow unchecked.

Neverthelesss, the fruits of organizational diffusion were not entirely counterproductive. Flexibility allowed the church to spread far from its home base and retain the character of an indigenous group. To people of non-Shona origin, the church still embodied aspects of important local practices, and it universally penalized witchcraft and sorcery in whatever idiom they arose. Faith healing and prophetic readings inspired by the Holy Spirit replaced various forms of traditional divination and curing. Although the official elders were appointed by the church center, every member of the church, whether confirmed at the Passover or not, had spiritual responsibilities. Unconfirmed women were generally considered healers and the men, evangelists. Their responsibilities in worship services and in work settings gained them indirect influence in church decisions and important positions of ceremonial management, regardless of whether they had participated in the Passover.

A highly centralized organization would never have tolerated the innovations that took place in the Maranke church. Its mode of diffusion differed from that of the related Apostolic Sabbath Church of God, or Masowe Apostles, which relied uniquely on cohesive missionary cadres sent directly from Zimbabwe to instruct and live among non-Shona-speaking groups.[16] As described previously, the Maranke group relied on the conversion of a local core of leaders, with a limited emphasis on culturally based heterodoxy. This gave an extraordinary flexibility to the church. For the Maranke Apostles as a whole, heterodoxy might be interpreted not so much in terms of personal preference and mobility as with respect to the freedom of the outlying congregations to appeal to local leaders. The only boundaries placed on these innovations were those of the annual sacrament. In its absence, the innovations so well anticipated by John Maranke could not be reviewed. The restriction that Apostolic members placed on heterodoxy was originally intended to be enforced through the annual "purification" of each *kerek*. For every commandment broken by individual members, the regional representatives, central leaders, and judges at the Passover invariably found spiritual solutions. But in the absence of such leaders or in conflicts

16. Kileff (1973:28, 35) stated that Masowe's group, also of Eastern Shona origin, has traveled to Zambia, Tanzania, Kenya, and the Zaire. Although their local congregations are growing rapidly in these locations, a small Shona-speaking missionary group is always sent ahead and resides in the new community for at least 2 years before moving to another area to proselytize.

over their jurisdiction, who could be left to judge? Could a centralized tribunal, separated by distance and political boundaries from the
sources of discord, deal with jealousies and mutual accusations in
outlying areas?

"SO MANY WITCHES": A MOUNTING LEADERSHIP CRISIS

When tensions among local leaders could not be easily resolved,
witchcraft accusations were raised as an aspect of political disputes.
Among Apostles, the possibility of witchcraft always appears in instances of anger, illness, doctrinal resistance, and transgression of
church laws. When splits threatened the integrity of established local
groups, leaders regularly introduced witchcraft as an explanation and
as a label for dissidents. To be valid, an accusation of witchcraft
among elders must be verified by a confirmed church prophet and
enforced by the open court (*dare*) at the church's center. This dual
verification makes it difficult for local leaders embroiled in a dispute
to make a viable witchcraft accusation on the international level. In
such cases, church leaders may ultimately abdicate their autonomy
to seek a visionary decision about a particular leader's culpability.
The tension between prophecy and leadership that arose in the
growth of the organization appeared again in the judgment of disputes, where visionary truths were sought as the basis of political
compromise. A direct ethnographic account of the witchcraft trials
will illustrate this problem.

As I walked by a group of about 80 men and women seated on
the ground in the Passover site, a friend pulled me by the arm and
whispered, "Have you ever seen so many witches, so many witches?"
I had just witnessed the beginning of the witchcraft trials and confessions at the Bocha Passover. Those accused were said to have trans-
gressed commandments and to have used witchcraft against members
of their families or other Apostles.[17] They were detected by prophets in the preworship visionary examination or *keti* ("gate") and
sent for trial to the evangelists. Not all accusations begin with the
prophets, and not all are based solely on personal injury or the visible
characteristics of the witch. The political rivalries described by an-
thropologists as the backdrop for many instances of sorcery and

17. Murphree (1969:105–108) presented a general description of the witchcraft accusations and confessions that precede the Passover ceremony. It must be added that witchcraft accusations may take place at any time and may be handled at regular Sabbath ceremonies as well as at the Passover.

witchcraft accusations are also part of the fabric of Apostolic witchcraft trials.[18] Although an Apostolic woman seeking traditional medicines rather than cure by faith may be labeled a sorceress, her case is generally settled by a single confession. However, an accusation born of rivalry, as already suggested, is more difficult to resolve.

In July of 1974 at the Bocha paschal trials, an accusation of extreme misconduct was lodged against the congregational leader Nawezi Petro and one of witchcraft against his former evanglist, Kadima Alphonse. From then on, the two men with graying beards, who nearly 20 years earlier had played such an important part in introducing the Apostolic Church to a foreign land, sat alone in the encampment. Occasionally, Nawezi could be seen opening a thin briefcase to extract newspapers recording his arrest and the recent history of the church from which, according to some accounts, he had just been expelled. His claim to be "the first cardinal" (founding Lieb-Umah) of Zaire had vanished along with the insignia of office worn on the front of his white uniform.

The growth of the outlying churches had led to some of the reasons behind Nawezi's trial. Their isolation from each other had created a crisis in leadership that each congregation looked to the central elders to resolve. In turn, these regional crises were compounded by Zimbabwean reactions to the death of John Maranke and the problems of succession at Bocha. There were a number of contradictory versions of each dispute. Immediately after Nawezi's case was judged, four different accounts of the verdict developed among church members with competing interests: (1) He had been expelled from the church. (2) He had not been expelled, but his rights to the office of head pastor or baptist Lieb-Umah had been suspended. (3) He was still an ordinary baptist (pastor), could attend ceremonies in that capacity, and would be reinstated as a Lieb-Umah within 2 months. (4) He was not an ordinary baptist but was still an Apostle and could attend ceremonies in that capacity. The first and fourth accounts were given by individuals at the church center and the second and third were held by Nawezi's supporters. In the absence of written records, all four oral reports could be treated as equally credible.

The background of Nawezi's case will now be placed in the context of the church's international organization. This case is essential to an understanding of the boundaries of Apostolic practice and the

18. Jones (1970:321–332, see especially p. 323) stated that in cases of political rivalry in a small village, witchcraft accusations are leveled at each other by the partisan followers. This process is not uncommon in sectarian accusations of witchcraft.

members' interpretations of organizational decisions. For this and similar instances of accusation, the discovery and interpretation of accepted verdicts is a task performed by each member involved. Sorting out multiple interpretations in order to produce an account of the church's organization is also a research problem that requires familiarity with the occasions on which decisions are made and enforced.

John's death in 1963 initially left the church with no definitive pattern for succession, although John had expressed the wish to see his eldest son become the leader. Simon, John's maternal cousin, and some of John's more distant relatives argued that the new leader should be chosen on a nonhereditary basis (Daneel 1971:331-339). As the special prophet who had always assisted John in delivering the sacrament, Simon proposed himself as the successor by virtue of his position as a paschal leader. He argued that John's belongings should be returned to the church rather than to John's immediate family. Even if Simon were not to become the leader, his position of power during the paschal tours would constitute a challenge to the new leadership's ability to centralize the church. Therefore, John's brother Anrod is said to have performed an Apostolic version of the traditional *kugadzira* or ancestor appeasement ceremony (Daneel 1971: 333-335). At this time, Abel ceremonially received his father's name of John the Baptist, his staff, his property, and his priestly responsibilities after the "unorthodox" traditional sacrifice of a sacred bull. Disgruntled, Simon left the church with a small number of followers. Rumors spread among Abel's followers accusing Simon of witchcraft. To the members of the outlying churches his departure had little meaning, and they did not support him.

Nawezi, however, was reluctant to accept Abel fully as a replacement for John. He referred to the then 30-year-old leader as "a child" and regarded himself as far more experienced. He was, nonetheless, anxious to usher the Passover into Zaire the year following John's death, and he made arrangements for Abel's trip. Abel was met in Lusaka by the Zambian leaders who escorted him to the Zairean border. Nawezi sent an emissary, his first evangelist Thomas, to accompany the leader to Lubumbashi for the ceremonies. Abel was dependent upon his hosts. He knew neither French nor the local languages and was unaware of the extent of the congregational divisiveness.

There are several accounts of the ensuing events. According to some members, Chisanga Luka, the head Zambian evangelist, and Kangwa William, the Zambian baptist, wanted to turn back. Someone was said to have deceived Abel by secretly telling the immigration authorities that his papers were incomplete. However, upon checking his papers, the immigration officials let Abel proceed. At a Passover 10 years later, Luka confessed his hesitancy about the plans to circumvent Abel. Nawezi's account was more emphatic. He claimed that his evangelist was intercepted by Musumbu with Luka's assistance and that Musumbu proceeded to escort Abel to his own paschal gathering, neglecting that of Nawezi. The following transcript is an excerpt from Nawezi's account, 2 years before his death.

> *Petro Nawezi, Lusaka, July 23, 1974:*
> The baptist [Abel] is waiting with the car and says to Luka, "Let's get on the road for the Congo." But my evangelist Lieb-Umah, Thomas, is there. He promised to go with the car to get him. When he heard these words, Musumbu went against me to go get him. Luka told him, "No, stop promising people, I have him, let's get on the road and go to the Congo. Where is the Congo? Nawezi's evangelist is here." When he said these words, he didn't believe him. Musumbu said, "Aah, let's go to the Congo. . . ."

As a reult of these incidents, Nawezi angrily contacted the police according to one account, although, from his own testimony, this story was constructed by the local government officials to cover their own mistake. Abel was arrested and then released. The police told him that Nawezi had ordered them to arrest and kill him. When Abel departed, he left behind the rift of schism. In Lubumbashi, there were three separate congregations, all, including Nawezi's, still claiming to fall under Abel's leadership: Musumbu's, Nawezi's, and Kadima's. In 1970, William Kangwa and the Zambian leadership tried to ease the situation by establishing a fourth congregation in Lubumbashi, consisting largely of Zambians, Zaireans, who had lived in Zambia, and Zimbabwean migrants. Should the Passover ever arrive again, each congregation would proclaim its legitimacy before Abel and insist on the right to a separate sacrament.

For many Zairean members, John's 1963 visit was the last sacrament performed. After the fiasco of 1964, Abel refused to make the journey to Zaire until the split was settled. The central leaders considered this an internal problem that they should not have to judge, while the Zairean leaders repeatedly appealed to Bocha to end the conflict. Meanwhile, Zairean Apostles attempted to make the journey to Bocha, but for most it was too difficult and costly. The Lubumbashi members worked out various techniques to adjust to a divisive situation. They attended different congregations each week, or, alternatively, became partisan supporters of a single group. Some of these divisions extended to other parts of Zaire. In the absence of comprehensive written records, and with the competing claims of different local leaders as to the attitude of the Zimbabwean elders, Zairean leaders repeatedly pressed for a definitive overarching decision from Bocha.

It is this situation that I encountered in 1971, shortly after my arrival in Zaire. In mid-September of that year, Nawezi sent a letter to Abel requesting the Passover ceremony in Zaire and assistance in unifying the church's fragmented congregations. I delivered this letter and became a witness to the negotiations between Nawezi and the Zimbabwean elders from that point onward. The letter was received by Makebi, Abel's younger brother. His reticent smile indicated that he considered Nawezi's request for sole authority invalid. Nawezi himself was summoned to confess before the Zimbabwean church. A return letter was addressed to Pierre Musumbu rather than Nawezi, tacitly recognizing Musumbu's authority in the situation. It questioned Musumbu concerning his name for the church and claim to national leadership. I was unable to understand why Nawezi had not received a direct reply to his communication. Nawezi presented himself as the chief elder and as the founder of the Zairean church. Although I had not taken seriously his claim to be a "cardinal," I thought that his letter deserved a direct response. From my position as a researcher and unwitting messenger, however, I felt that I was powerless to intervene.

The reply to Musumbu summoned him to Bocha. Subsequent letters called all of the Zairean leaders to be judged. Nawezi had accused Musumbu of unjustly usurping authority over all of the Zairean congregations. Musumbu, in turn, was said by many Apostles to have received a special insignia from John Maranke, a 12-pointed star like that worn by John himself. Members of the opposition group accused Musumbu of having fabricated the insignia without authorization to mystify the Zairean followers. For John and his sons, the ephod conferred the right to administer the Passover. John had not given Musumbu this prerogative but was said to have recognized him as the principal spiritual leader of Zaire. There were those who bellieved that Musumbu could, under certain circumstances, deliver the Passover. To my knowledge, Musumbu had never asserted this. During my research, I had heard Nawezi's story repeatedly: Musumbu had deceived the central leaders into acknowledging his congregation rather than Nawezi's when the paschal centers were established in the Zaire. Musumbu was the holder of the ephod while Nawezi had claimed to be the national founder and the first cardinal. Neither view was fully substantiated by the Zimbabwean center.

During the same period, the Zairean congregations were having organizational problems that made their appeal to the central hierarchy more pressing. In December 1971, when laws were passed curtailing worship among the majority of indigenous churches in the Zaire (*Aurore* 1972), each regional group needed the support and recognition of a single national leader in order to apply to the government for reinstatement as a recognized religious body. The Maranke Apostles were initially excluded from a list of 79 officially approved spirit churches and were later partially reinstated on a regional basis in Zaire (*Taïfa* 1972). Their international African hierarchy made them a special case, neither immediately welcomed as were the European churches nor free from the suspicion directed toward some of the local indigenous groups. In response, the Apostles sent competing delegations as their spokesmen to the Kinshasa authorities. Each delegation attempted to arm itself with letters and official statements attesting to its authority from the Zimbabwean leadership.

The necessity to present a unified picture to external agencies brought the intercongregational problems of leadership under secular review. A Kasaian congregation joined Nawezi to plead that Musumbu's status be decided once and for all. Was he, as he claimed, the Apostolic "representative" for the entire Zaire or were other paschal centers directly responsible only to Bocha? The issue of congregational unification was directly related to the church's accountability to national authorities. With either Musumbu or Nawezi as the church's representative, a single Zairean church could claim autonomous control over all of its branches.

Kadima and Nawezi joined in the criticism of Musumbu's presumed authority, but they continued to keep their own congregations separate. Informants asserted that this tacit alliance was one of the reasons for accusing Kadima of witchcraft. When government pressures relaxed and worship was resumed normally in Lubumbashi, Nawezi claimed that his delegation had been responsible for the favorable change. By the time that the accounts of the Zaire's troubles reached Bocha, all of the Zairean leaders were called for review. No complaints would be acknowledged until all accusers had stood before the open court at the Maranke reserve, for only prophets could determine "purity of heart" and the elder judges decide the official verdict of guilt or innocence.

"WHICH ONE OF THESE MEN IS TELLING THE TRUTH?" THE PROPHETIC RESOLUTION OF DISPUTES

Apostolic prophets claim to detect members' transgressions at a prophetic examination or gate (*keti*).[19] John Maranke, the founding prophet, was able to detect sin and he initiated the practice. Thereafter, anyone confirmed as a prophet by the other prophets and elders could conduct the *keti*, the content of which stands as evidence for any court case. While their judgments rely in part on the daily actions and reputations of members, final decisions are considered to emerge through spiritual inspiration. Impressive displays of true inspiration, as opposed to personal judgments, are often built into the *keti* performance. They include vivid prophecies by persons who do not know the candidate and the corroboration of independent verdicts by several prophets.

Once prophets have prayed over a case, the member judged guilty is referred either to one evangelist or to a tribunal of several. In Zimbabwe, these evangelists conducted two open courts for the duration of the Passover conference, and it was in the upper of these courts that the case of the Zairean leaders was heard. The lower court heard domestic cases and lesser witchcraft accusations.

Abraham, Abel's eldest son and a potential head of the church, watched the proceedings intently. Musumbu presented his case eloquently in fluent Chishona with full documentation of each event, just as he had done the day before. On that day, he had stood before the central tribunal with Nawezi. He had described the moment at which he had escorted Abel across the Zairean border in 1964 and had announced his grievances against Nawezi. Now, he was before the tribunal with Kadima to end the struggle for leadership. Musumbu essentially wished to clarify his position as the main intermediary between Zaire and the Zimbabwean center. Kadima, the last of the major leaders who had challenged Musumbu's claim, was now standing with him in court contesting Musumbu's accusation of misconduct and witchcraft and accusing him in turn of trying to oust him from the church. As Kadima defended himself, an 11-year-old boy asked one of the judges with genuine curiosity: "Which one of those

19. The prophetic examination is a dramatic event. One or two prophets speak "in tongues" and prophesy over each Apostle before each worship event and before the paschal ceremony. If the member is found to be "in sin," he/she is sent to confess to an evangelist or to the *dare* (group of evangelists). Descriptions of the *keti* are contained in Jules-Rosette (1975); Murphree (1969:106); and Aquina (1967:203–219, especially p. 207).

men is telling the truth?'' The judge smiled at the question that he would help to arbitrate but could never resolve.

Two members were called into the *dare* to discuss the Musumbu-Kadima debate. They prayed and presented the visionary solutions that they had received. The first member was a confirmed prophet and the second a baptist who was said to have a reputation for honesty. Field notes for that afternoon summarize the event.

July 20, 1974: The Prophecies:
Account #1:
Praying strongly several times between each statement, the prophet presented four verdicts on the dispute between Musumbu and Kadima.

1. "I see a tug of war between them." Both men assented to this with "Amen."
2. "In the middle I see a woman." They again replied, "Amen."
3. Their argument involves this woman." Their response was "Amen."
4. "It is a case of adultery to be decided." To this they said, "no."

Account #2:
Then the baptist came forward. He stood next to Chief Maranke's son, who was the head evangelist in the case, and presented a prophetic verdict. His statement, as translated by one of the judges, was as follows:

The Baptist sees in a vision the same tug of war as the prophet. He says that Musumbu wants Kadima, the evangelist, to obey him. Kadima, on the other hand, feels that Musumbu hates him and does not want him in the church. This is the reason, according to Kadima, that the accusation of witchcraft was made. Kadima replied, "Amen."

Why are they fighting? The vision shows Musumbu picking up sand and throwing it on people. He must be very careful not to follow behind people and worry about what they are doing and must look after his own affairs, or he will find himself back in this same court. The vision shows Kadima with a blackboard on which four things are written. He agrees to the first three but not to the fourth. It is this same matter of witchcraft. He sees Kadima walking in the mud. When he came out, he left footprints on the ground. He should confess.

In the vision, Kadima appears to be arguing with a man in his village who is not an Apostle. He must be aware lest he become like a man going out to sow corn with only a few grains in it. The evangelist has two matters that he should confess. The baptist who was prophesying repeated the words, "Confess, confess."

Kadima confessed that the dispute was over Musumbu's accusation of witchcraft. Musumbu, he claimed, could not accuse an evangelist of witchcraft, a baptist of witchcraft and a prophet of witchcraft.

Discussion followed. As a part of his argument that Musumbu had falsely accused him to the Zairean government, Kadima presented a Zairean newspaper article in which Musumbu's picture was identified as Muchabaya Sithole (Abel) and Abel's as Musumbu. The article contained an account of Apostolic medical policy, stating that members were allowed to go to the hospital, a practice counter to church regulations. Although Kadima wanted the entire article to be read, excerpts were translated from French into English for the *dare*. A second article was also excerpted. It contained a list of leaders, including Kadima, who had been expelled from the church for gross misconduct and negligence of church regulations. The article stated that a new committee of elders had been named.

The Resolution
Account #1: (a judge's translation of the proceedings):
The judges tried to coax Musumbu and Kadima to reach an agreement concerning the matter of witchcraft. No conclusion was reached. A decision was made that the two should go out for the night, think about the dispute, and try to make an agreement when they returned.

Account #2:
A judge summarized the final verdict for Musumbu's case in answer to my questions. He stated: "Nawezi and Kadima are still Apostles, but they are no longer Lieb-Umahs (high leaders). This is because of the arrest in 1964. Musumbu doesn't want them to come to Bocha. That's why he said that they are no longer Apostles. But the law of the church says that if a person does something, he should confess it. Nawezi should have confessed right after the arrest, in Bocha or anywhere. But he didn't come until now."

Diverse accounts of a scene were combined to produce a unified picture of the Zairean leadership. The young boy's bewilderment as to who was telling the truth was ultimately handled as a matter of practical management. However, the most definitive aspects of the negotiation were presented in the form of visionary solutions. The impact of the spiritual resolution far exceeds that of other statements for Apostles. Haldor Heimer has summarized this tendency among the Zairean Apostles:

> The leaders often become preoccupied with heavenly visions so that they are removed and withdrawn from the present problems which surround the faithful. It is thus that the Bapostolo [the Apostles], in a kind of passive resignation, receive certain compensations in the form of ritual, song, dress, and visions without relating themselves to the outside world (1971:367).

The visionary solutions presented to the *dare* were contested by both members under the assumption that only information verified as spiritually true by the accused can be accepted. This process of verification involves the practical assessment of any given account and the negotiation of competing accounts into a solution or "reality" acceptable to the participants.

Whereas in many cases, one would expect a practical resolution to preclude any statements that might be extraordinary or visionary, Apostles seek the prophetic solution. It is through the prophetic solution that a spiritually verified assembly of multiple and contradictory accounts of a single incident can be made. However, the fact that a spiritual rendition of an event exists does not assure the "truth" of that description nor does it preclude competing accounts. Rather, several underlying conditions are present. The participants assess each other personally. Thus, both prophetic decisions and personal insertions must be determined as fitting into one or the other category. The reliability of the prophet must be determined, with every possibility that his effectiveness in this particular case can be challenged on personal grounds. Acceptance of the relevance of visionary descriptions is a prerequisite for the judgments. So too is the recognition that these descriptions may be inadequate to bring about a final resolution from the judges and the parties themselves. In the last analysis, the competing accounts are negotiated through a subtle "politics of belief."[20]

Both parties in the case denied portions of the prophecies. The prophets themselves presented different particulars but agreed on the overall definition of the problem. The judges accepted neither the participants' nor the prophets' solutions in full but gave Musumbu and Kadima time to "think over" the resolution of the case most acceptable to them. Abel, under whose jurisdiction the final matter would be resolved and who would give ultimate legitimacy to the *dare* decision, placed his trust in the prophetic decision. Abel stressed that even he had to pass though the *keti* examination and was ultimately subject to the *law of the prophets*. The decision's acceptance, particularly by the plaintiff, was problematic, and its main features (i.e., some combination of both prophecies) could be enforced only if Kadima and Musumbu were in accord.

20. Cf. Pollner (1973: especially pp. 2–5), who argued that the election of one interpretation as definitive, rather than a competing one, is a conscious choice or act of commitment. Electing one underlying assumption and portraying it as real or true is merely an assertion, a part of the "politics" of belief and experience.

Accounts of the resolution were equally diverse. At that time, it seemed that all sides were pleased. Prophecy had triumphed in locating witchcraft as an issue but not in identifying a witch. Each side interpreted its party as winning. Musumbu denied that Kadima and Nawezi were full church members, while Nawezi himself persisted in describing the decision as a temporary "demotion" that would be rectified in a few months' time. When the decision was not reversed, Nawezi later rejected it altogether. The way in which Nawezi and Kadima told these stories to their congregations introduced even more variations in the decision. Several months after the decision, Nawezi stood by his account and refused the judgment from Bocha.

Are these multiple resolutions a sign of heterodoxy and heteropraxy? Do they indicate a failure of political centralization? Rather than answer these questions definitively, I would suggest that the accepted solution is negotiated on individual occasions under the ideal pattern suggested by Abel. Spiritual interpretations, rather than being handled as illusory, are given primacy but not accepted without the practical concurrence of those present. Even when a negotiated solution is reached, its interpretation is bounded by a specific context and may take on widely differing meanings as the congregational leadership changes.[21]

Two years after the Bocha decision on Nawezi and Kadima, Nawezi died in Lubumashi. Up to this time, he continued to hold full worship services with his congregation. He wore the Lieb-Umah insignia and resisted efforts to label him as suspended or expelled. Nawezi made no further claims to full control of the Zairean church. However, he refused to recognize that he was not the primary leader in charge of all of the Lubumbashi congregations. He and Kadima effected a reconciliation and continued to share congregation members who would alternate between their worship services. Nawezi's death left his followers in questionable circumstances. Many of them sought support and full reinstatement through the Zambian branch of the church. As late as June of 1978, Kadima continued with his attempts to denounce Musumbu, sending a two-page letter with biblical passages in both English and French to all outlying congregations. Kadima stated that the purpose of his letter was to assure that

21. The position of an entire account in this case resembles that of a context-bound expression in semantics. These "indexical expressions" include such words as "this," "that," and "it," that gain their meaning only through the context of use. All linguistic expressions may be regarded in a more general sense as relying on their context for the conversant's interpretation of intended meaning (Bar-Hillel 1954:359–379; Garfinkel and Sacks 1970: 338–366, especially pp. 348–350).

law and order prevailed in all of the outlying branches of the church. Meanwhile, the increasingly difficult political situation in Zimbabwe made communication with the central elders fragmentary. Their ability to enforce any ecclesiastic sanctions outside of Zimbabwe was virtually neutralized. Individual leaders continued to invoke actual and presumed communications with Zimbabwe as legitimate organizational support for local congregational charges. As a result, the prognosis for the future of the Apostles as a centralized group became more uncertain in the long term after the Musumbu–Nawezi–Kadima decision.

A NEW CHURCH

The problematic character of the Musumbu–Nawezi–Kadima case raises a general organizational issue for the Apostles. How would the outlying churches be regulated in the absence of the Passover centralization? Cultural variation in ritual, internal schism, and competing claims to leadership complicate matters. The judgment for Musumbu, although somewhat ambiguous, set a precedent for a national spokesman and leader for parts of the church outside of Bocha. But, the criteria on which this decision was made combined differing claims about spiritual legitimacy with the expedient management of a case. It is difficult to assess to what extent Zairean Apostles accepted Musumbu's claim to be the chief intermediary and regional head of the church. Some Apostles regarded this explanation as the only possibility, while others preferred to keep any disagreement secret for fear of being pinpointed for expulsion, accusation of witchcraft, or at the least, malice. Still others sang topical songs with political commentaries to the tunes of spiritually inspired hymns.

Nawezi and Kadima continued to retain their followings until Nawezi's death and remained firm about both their accounts of and repentance for the rift in the 1960s. They wanted reinstatement after confession of their old grievances, and some of the leaders at Bocha supported them. Without reinstatement, they continued to cling to the hope that the challenge to them was only temporary. When Nawezi died in 1976, the split had not yet been healed. Musumbu subsequently named Nawezi's nephew a regional leader in an attempt at unification, but mutual hostility remained. Kadima's separate position was unchanged.

The church has now expanded, not only to Mozambique, Malawi, and other African locations, but also potentially beyond

Africa.[22] For Mozambique, the challenge of a leader to hold the 12-starred insignia has resulted in a clean break from Bocha. The center's contact with these areas remains indirect. It is possible that Musumbu's case will be the precedent for the establishment of a new church, one in which more regional autonomy will be acknowledged as well as required. Musumbu's appeal and ability to unify several congregations may result in a new type of institutional arrangement in which the founding church relies more fully on a national council of elders to resolve the problems of regional congregations. This process has already begun in the Zaire. Yet, Apostles at the church's center and its outlying branches will always consider these possibilities to rely upon a delicate balance maintained between the church's peripheral branches and prophecy and leadership at the center.

CONCLUSIONS

This case study in schism and continuity illustrates the Apostles' reliance on visionary solutions to social problems. Visionary solutions establish a "correct" version of a dispute even if the resolution is not enforced. Church leaders also invoke visionary solutions when other forms of compromise do not work. In examining the roots of international growth among the Apostles, it is possible to conclude that their leaders shared the following assumptions: (1) The Apostolic church is international. (2) The Zimbabwean church is the center and its leaders can stand in judgment of all others. (3) Certain regional leaders may also be selected as intermediaries to the Zimbabwean center. (4) All disputes can ultimately be described and resolved through prophetic inspiration.

These assumptions betray an underlying conflict between prophecy and leadership. Although all leaders are subject to prophetic review, they may challenge spiritual decisions. Personal assertions of power can be used to reinterpret prophecies and even invalidate them interactionally. Furthermore, the prophecies contain a typical or idealized version of events that may be ignored as well as reinterpreted in the context of everyday activities. The founding center's prophetic control is localized. The more removed the outlying churches are from the Zimbabwean center, the more difficult it becomes for the leaders there to receive news of these congregations

22. Both Britons and Americans have been baptized as members, although few of the non-African congregations seem to have retained an active commitment to the group.

and to enforce both visionary and practical judgments about them. Although rendering a prophetic judgment does not require the presence of those involved, the judgment cannot be acted upon without their direct confession to church leaders and face-to-face testimony.

The gap between prophecy and leadership, the ambiguities stemming from interpretations of events by rival and distant factions, and the continuation of a pattern of missionizing in reverse may well result in a "new" Apostolic church that differs greatly in accepted doctrine and practice from John's original vision. Whether or not far-reaching changes occur, the relationship between the expanding congregations and the church center will remain a complex aspect of organizational growth.

By examining the ways in which church members assemble diverse accounts of key events and descriptions of what they interpret as a crisis in leadership, it is possible to present Apostolic beliefs as a dynamic "living theology," rather than an idealized set of practices.[23] Such an analysis of the Apostles and, potentially, of other religious movements, focuses on the relationship between spiritual and practical decisions, on the tension between prophecy and leadership in ceremonial and everyday events. In an organization that retains a personal model of leadership, it is necessary to examine the politics of belief that arise among individual perspectives in the light of larger organizational tendencies toward continuity and change.

REFERENCES

Aquina, Sister Mary, O.P. 1967 "The People of the Spirit: An Independent Church in Rhodesia," *Africa*, 37, 2 (April):203–219.
Aurore 1972 Une Décision Salvatrice Pour le Kasai Occidental, January 20–25.
Bar-Hillel, Yehoshua 1954 "Indexical Expressions," *Mind*, 63:359–379.
Barrett, D. B. 1968 *Schism and Renewal in Africa: An Analysis of Six Thousand Contemporary Religious Movements.* Nairobi: Oxford Univerity Press.
Daneel, M. L. 1971 *The Background and Rise of Southern Shona Independent Churches.* The Hague: Mouton.
Essor du Congo 1956 Interdiction d'une secte indigène au Katanga. November 12.
Garfinkel, H. and H. Sacks 1970 "On Formal Structures of Practical Actions," in *Theoret-*

---

23. Siman (1971:18), in describing the early Christian church at Antioch, stresses the critical importance of liturgy as a reflection of doctrine and belief. To liturgy, I would add all interactions relevant to ritual performance. The combination of these interactions and ritual performance constitutes a "living theology" in contrast to an extracted and idealized conception of a movement's orthodox beliefs.

ical Sociology, Edward Tiryakian and John McKinney, eds. New York: Appleton-Century-Crofts.

Goffard, J. 1958 Compte Rendue de la Réunion Tenue le 30.8.58 au Bureau du Territoire entre M. L'Administrateur du Territoire Pepin et Kasanda Vincent, Prophète de l'Apostolic Church. September 2.

Heimer, H. 1971 "The Kimbanguists and the Bapostolo: A Study of Two African Independent Churches in Luluabourg, Congo in Relation to Similar Churches and in the Context of Lulua Traditional Culture and Religion." Unpublished Ph.D. dissertation, Hartford Seminary Foundation.

Hentgen, E. F. 1958 Letter from Territorial Administrator, No. 46, April 17.

Hentgen, E. F. 1959 Letter No. 26/31, April 20.

Jones, G. I. 1970 "A Boundary to Accusations." In Mary Douglas, ed., *Witchcraft Confessions and Accusations.* London: Tavistock Publications.

Jules-Rosette, B. 1975 *African Apostles: Aspects of Ritual and Conversion in the Church of John Maranke.* Ithaca: Cornell University Press.

Jules-Rosette, B. 1976 "The Mushecho: A Girls' Purity Rite." Paper and videotape presented at the 7th Annual Conference on Visual Anthropology, Temple University.

Jules-Rosette, B. 1977 "Grass-Roots Ecumenism: Religious and Social Cooperation in Two African Churches," *African Social Research,* 23:185–216.

Kileff, M. 1973 *The Apostolic Sabbath Church of God: Ritual, Organization and Belief.* Unpublished manuscript, University of Tennessee, Chattanooga.

Lemborelle, J. 1958 Letter from the Governor of Kasai, No. 221/00833, February 26.

Maranke, J. 1953 *The New Witness of the Apostles.* Bocha: Mimeographed.

Mayer, P. 1961 *Townsmen or Tribesmen.* Cape Town: Oxford University Press.

Moriame, E. 1950 Province du Katanga. Arrêté No. 21/149 du novembre 1956 interdisant l'activité de la secte "Apostolic Church."

Murphree, M. W. 1969 *Christianity and the Shona.* London: The Athlone Press.

Pollner, M. 1973 "The Very Coinage of your Brain: The Resolution of Reality Disjunctures." Unpublished paper, UCLA.

Rutten 1926 Gouverneur General. Ordonnance du 11 février 1926 No. 14/Cont. relative aux associations indigènes dans les centres européens.

Siman, Emmanuel Pataq 1971 *L'Experience de l'Esprit par l'Eglise.* Paris: Beauchesne.

Taïfa 1972 79 Communautés Religieuses Reconnues au Zaire. May 2.

Tshibangu, G. T. 1970 Histoire de l'apparition de l'Eglise Apostolique Africain Church dans la République Démocratique du Congo. Unpublished report. Lubumbashi.

V

George C. Bond

A PROPHECY THAT FAILED
The Lumpa Church of Uyombe, Zambia[1]

I

Religious movements founded by Africans who claim Christianity as the source of their inspiration are a marked feature of contemporary Africa. The assumption that the movements arose in response to European colonial domination has tended to obscure the fact that many of the basic conditions which Balandier describes as constituting the "colonial situation" (Balandier 1966:pp. 54-55), and which have been conducive to the rise and proliferation of prophetic movements, may still obtain even after African countries have gained

1. This chapter is based on actual fieldwork in 1964–1965 among members of the Uyombe Lumpa Congregation in Uyombe and Isoka. The District Commissioner kindly allowed me extensive visitation rights of Lumpa during their confinement with the understanding that I would not publish the more dramatic aspects of my observations for several years and even then I should use discrete judgment. I have sought to comply fully with our understanding. I wish to thank the Zambia Government and its representatives as well as local authorities and Lumpa for their cooperation. I also wish to thank the National Endowment for the Humanities for a summer grant which provided me with the time to work on this chapter and volume.

AFRICAN CHRISTIANITY
Patterns of Religious Continuity

their political independence. The economic conditions established during colonial rule and the socioeconomic position of most Africans may not change; Africans' freedom of political and religious expression may be controlled and even more restricted than under colonial rule. In one phase of its development a prophetic movement may be or may appear to be anticolonial and anti-European, but in another it may become apparent that its opposition was and is to secular authorities, whether European or African. This demonstrates the limitation of religious typologies. Inevitably, they freeze a reality which is in flux, and their mechanical application may seriously distort any dialectical analysis of historical process. That these religious movements are in constant flux points to the difficulty of attempting to designate their specific political dimensions. Nonetheless, the emphasis placed on their political orientation has called attention to the conditions conducive to their widespread acceptance by Africans, more especially peasants and wage earners.

I think it may be fair to argue that many African prophetic movements are part of the complex historical processes that are contributing to what may be termed the making of an African "common people." Although Hobsbawm uses the term "common people" to refer to precapitalist societies, I think it may also be used to capture the nature of new social formations and consciousness of precapitalist societies experiencing new modes of capitalist production which both transcend and incorporate the peasantry of the countryside and the laboring poor of the towns. Hobsbawm's formulation is that "there will frequently be not high or low 'classness', but, in the sense of consciousness, no 'classness' at all, beyond the miniature scale. Alternatively, it may be suggested, the unity felt by the subaltern groups will be so global as to go beyond class and state. There will not be peasants, but 'people' or 'countrymen'; there will be not workers, but an indiscriminate 'common people' or 'labouring poor'. . . [Hobsbawm 1972: p. 10]."

The gradual transformation of precapitalist societies to capitalism has brought African peasants and wage earners into new alignments which transcend their parochial and particularistic affiliations and unite them with others as part of the subaltern classes. The phase in which a "common people" may be discerned is possibly a prelude to, and may even be a neccessary condition for, the emergence of a modern class society and class consciousness. Under colonial rule the process began whereby most African agricultural "tribesmen" were to be transformed into peasants and proletarians, but they also be-

came, in Hobsbawm's sense, part of a common people. Marx regarded the French peasantry as consisting of isolated units of consumption, and stated that they constituted a class only in that their
economic conditions put them in hostile opposition to other classes
(Marx 1975: p. 124). That is to say, although the French peasantry
of the mid-nineteenth century could be viewed as a class, their degree
of class consciousness was extremely low. Marx's view of the peasantry as a class with a low degree of consciousness should be distin-
guished from Hobsbawm's view of a common people, a view which
I feel more accurately characterizes part of a historical phase through
which many African populations are passing. The notion of a common people does not however negate objective class formation but
attempts to capture a dimension of a historical process which in
many instances has given rise to classes. But a population such as the
Yombe of Zambia are neither peasants nor proletarians—or rather
they are both—so they cannot be expected to demonstrate class
consciousness (consciousness of *peasants as a class,* or *proletarians as
a class*). Instead what they exhibit is the more diffuse consciousness
of a common laboring people, and it is this feature that makes them
eminently receptive to new religious movements. Put differently,
new social formations such as the rise of a common people produce
new ideological forms. The class awareness of the laboring poor was
often embodied in and expressed through new religious movements.
These religions of the common people subverted the possibility of
class consciousness and reinforced the diffuse awareness of a tenu-
ously shared social allegiance.

In this chapter I intend to look not only at the social situation
in which a branch or congregation of a prophetic movement, the
Lumpa Church of Alice Lenshina Mulenga, arose but also at its religious character and orientation. I intend to suggest that the Uyombe
congregation was reformist in that it sought a return to the fundamentalist teachings of early mission Christianity and that it was not
oriented toward reestablishing the traditional culture and beliefs of
the Yombe. Rather, it directly opposed them. The name of the
Church, Lumpa, which means "the strong, the most important"
(Oger 1962:p. 133) suggests but does not fully capture the righteous
Christian fervor which was to develop among Alice Lenshina's followers and the concerted effort which they were to make to set themselves apart from their indigenous societies, from the social order
produced under colonial rule and the one promised by the United
National Independence Party (U.N.I.P.), the principal and today the

only political party of Zambia. The new social order to which members of the Lumpa Church aspired was based upon Christian principles.

II

The Lumpa Church arose during a period of growing political unrest in Zambia. In 1953 the British territories of what are today known as Zambia, Malawi, and Southern Rhodesia were incorporated in the Federation of Rhodesia and Nyasaland, against the wishes of the African population. The Federation was opposed not only by the African political elites of the urban areas, but also by the traditional elites in the country. The early 1950s were marked by widespread discontent and a growing political awareness. In addition, the postwar economic boom in the mining industries was tapering off, with fluctuations in the opportunities for African employment (Barber 1961:p. 228). Although it was not until the late 1950s, the years during which the Lumpa Church reached its peak and U.N.I.P. was founded, that there was marked decline in employment opportunities for Africans, nonetheless the erratic nature of the labor market, combined with the unpredictable political situation, produced uncertainty and insecurity, particularly in economically depressed areas such as the Northern Province.

The dominant ethnic group of the Northern Province is the Bemba, who are noted more for their tradition as warriors than as cultivators. With the opening of the copper mines they entered the labor market as labor migrants. It was among them that in 1953 Alice Lenshina arose as a prophet and from them that she recruited her most loyal adherents. Social conditions in the Northern Province were conducive to the emergence and acceptance of a prophetic message and the founding of a new independent church, or spiritual community, which could provide some degree of security and certainty in the context of rapid political and economic change. Not only did the Lumpa Church provide such security, it also gave protection against traditional beliefs concerning the causes of misfortune. Roberts perceptively noted that it "was heir to two traditions in the modern history of Zambia: movements toward African Christian independence, and movements toward the eradication of witchcraft and sorcery [1970: p. 516]." For him, the Lumpa Church was a syncretic movement, "mingling elements of belief and practice which were European and African in origin [1970: p. 515]." Although this observation may have been true of some Lumpa congregations, it would not be entirely appropriate in characterizing the one found in Uyombe chiefdom. It is not the syncretic aspect of the movement that is important, but the new synthesis that it represents. The Yombe congregation thought that membership in the church was itself sufficient to protect them from witchcraft and sorcery. Witchcraft and sorcery were now interpreted as a part of the struggle between God and Satan for the soul of Man. A new social form was in the making, one which on the one hand was a synthesis but on the other hand, the antithesis of traditional Yombe beliefs. Moreover, the Lumpa Church did not recognize ancestor worship and, hence, the belief in ancestors as a cause of misfortunes. It offered to its members an alternative way to gain control over the forces harmful to man. It also prohibited many traditional customs and practices. Its rules and doctrines laid the foundations for a multiethnic religious movement which was not just a church but a spiritual community opposed to secular authority.

Roberts has written an excellent general account of the growth of the Lumpa Church in Zambia. Thus, I need only describe selected features of the larger movement as a background to a discussion of the Yombe congregation. The Lumpa Church was founded by Alice Lenshina Mulenga, a barely literate Bemba woman from Chinsali District in the Northern Province. In 1953 she had a spiritual experience, one which conforms to an established and now expected pattern among the Bantu-speaking peoples of Central and Southern Africa (Sundkler 1961). She claimed that she experienced death and was transported to heaven. While she was dead, she met with a Christian spirit, which has been described variously as Jesus, angels, or God (Rotberg 1961: p.66), who taught her, informed her of the power of hymns, and gave her a new Christian text which was supposed to embody the true message of God and was intended for Africans. She was then returned to earth with the mission of carrying out God's works. She was also instructed to go to the Presbyterian missionaries at Lubwa Mission in Chinsali, to relate her experience to them, and to continue her training to become a member of the United Church of Central Africa, the Zambian designation of the Presbyterian Free Church of Scotland.

In 1954 Alice Mulenga left Lubwa, established herself at Kasomo village and began to teach her gospel, drawing large crowds. At first, Lubwa missionaries looked favorably on her activities and visited her at Kasomo (Robert 1970: pp. 523–524). But it soon became apparent that she was straying from the Free Church. She began calling upon sorcerers to give up their evil practices and to baptize those who came with their troubles into her church. Hers was an ethical prophecy, not an exemplary one (Weber 1965: p. 55). She imposed moral precepts on her followers and although she allowed some of them to preach, she remained the ultimate source of authority. Only she performed the critical rite of baptism, and most appointments to church posts required her personal approval. The Movement drew members from both Presbyterian and Catholic Churches, from different ethnic groups, from both matrilineal and patrilineal peoples and from a range of social statuses. Not only did many chiefs support it, but village headmen and the ordinary villager joined it. Taylor and Lehmann estimate that by the end of 1955 about 60,000 persons had visited Kasomo (1961:p. 226). The Movement spread rapidly through the Northern and Eastern Provinces and along the line of rail into the urban centers.

The prophetic experience of Alice Mulenga, although expressed through the traditional idiom of spirit possession, was based upon belief in the efficacy of Christian spirits. There were two dimensions to her prophecy, one general and the other particular. The general dimensions were those that she shared with other prophets. The nature of her prophetic experiences places her within the context of other prophets of the region. Hymns, for example, are believed to put the prophet in the proper spiritual condition to receive the powers of Christian spirits. (For a thorough analysis of the role of hymns in an African Church see Jules-Rosette, 1975). The general features help to make the prophecy acceptable and provide it with legitimacy. The particular dimension refers to the idiosyncratic elements in her teaching. Alice Lenshina's practice of having those just baptized turn their backs while she retreated behind a large tree, played the flute, and conversed with God is an example of her particular style (Oger 1962: p. 130). But the cultural idiom must not be confused with the social or religious substance. It serves only as the medium of the message and may obscure the underlying structure of the Movement. Alice's spiritual experience and her style were syncretic and personal but the moral prohibitions of the Lumpa Church demonstrate a close affiliation to the early fundamentalist teachings of the mission Christianity of the Free Church. It prohibited a number of activities such as adultery, polygyny, and divorce, and dancing, drinking, and smoking in a sacred area, as well as the practice of witchcraft and sorcery (Taylor and Lehmann 1961: p. 253). Members were expected to have their marriages performed in the Church and their disputes judged by Church officers. Increasingly, they regarded themselves as above the jurisdiction of civil authorities, responsible only to the Church, its officers, and its founder. The Movement stood outside politics in the sense that members were not allowed to join a political party. By 1959 the Lumpa Church had about 148 congregations, most of which were distributed in Chinsali District and other rural areas; 132 congregations were in the Northern and Eastern Provinces and 16 in the urban centers (Roberts 1970: p. 535). The membership was estimated at between 50,000 and 100,000. The Church had not only grown in size, but also displayed considerable wealth in its fleet of trucks and cars and its monumental Church at Kasomo, the spiritual center of the Movement. The Movement had reached its peak.

As the Lumpa Church grew in strength it increasingly lost contact with the political changes that were shaping Zambia and moving it toward independence. In 1959 U.N.I.P. was founded under the leadership of Kenneth Kaunda, who was himself from Chinsali and whose father was a prominent evangelist of the Free Church and a teacher at Lubwa Mission. U.N.I.P. was intended to be a mass political party and quickly set about founding branches throughout the Northern and Eastern Provinces. The Lumpa Church had already antagonized the chiefs by refusing to recognize their authority. They readily gave their support to U.N.I.P., as did many headmen and common folk. The Lumpa church, however, refused to allow its members to join in the struggle for independence. The scene was set for a major struggle between U.N.I.P. and the Lumpa Church, a struggle which erupted into widespread violence in July 1964, and which lasted through October, claiming the lives of well over 700 people (Report 1965). The Lumpa were defeated, the Church was banned by the Government, and its members were imprisoned.

III

To my knowledge there are very few detailed accounts of local congregations of the Lumpa Church, and even in Roberts' excellent study of the Movement, there is no description of the structure of a congregation and the beliefs of its members. He recognizes that the reasons for the success or failure of the Lumpa Church in any particular area could only be discovered by a study of local conditions (Roberts 1970: p. 536). In this section I intend to describe the Yombe congregation against the background of the larger Lumpa movement and within the local context.

I have elsewhere described some of the basic features of Yombe society (Bond 1972, 1976). Here I intend to present only a brief overview. The Yombe, a Bantu-speaking people, are sparsely distributed over an area of some 625 square miles in Isoka District in the Northern Province of Zambia. A small branch of the Tumbuka, who live in the Northern Province of Malawi, they number about 11,000, or 14% of the total population of Isoka District. Land within the chiefdom is fertile and more than plentiful for the cultivation of the three main crops: maize, millet, and beans. But there are few opportunities for local wage employment. For more than 50 years Yombe men have engaged in labor migration and at any one time from 25 to 35% of the men are absent (living abroad) from the chiefdom. These figures on labor migration do not however reflect the range within the chiefdom. The northeastern part of Uyombe has the highest rate of labor migration, ranging as high as 40% of the adult male taxpaying population. This is an area of few roads, remote from the main commercial center and capital, Muyombe, of the chiefdom in the south. Since the turn of the century the Yombe have been exposed to Christianity and mission training. They could attend Free Church mission schools at Livingstonia in Malawi and Lubwa and Mwenzo in Zambia. In the 1920s the Livingstonia mission established several schools in the south, but only one in the northeastern part of the chiefdom, at Kalinda Village which was closed in 1927 when its head teacher, John Punyira Wowo, became chief of Uyombe. But despite the lack of school education this region was fully familiar with the fundamentalist teachings of mission Christianity. Christian and Western norms and values, beliefs and practices, are, then, in no way alien to the Yombe.

Indigenous government in Uyombe was based upon the recognition of a chief. Spatially defined units, villages, were each under a headman. Although the chief appointed headmen, he did not have the right to dismiss them without the approval and consent of a council composed of the prominent men of the six branches of the royal clan. This council reserved the right to review his decisions on matters such as chiefdom citizenship and village boundaries. The royal clan was the owner of the chiefdom, its land, its people, and the chieftainship, and its most prominent and powerful members were the headmen of the central villages of its branches, who were selected by the royal clan and not by the chief. The royal clan gave the chiefdom a coherent political framework, while its council provided a check on the chief's powers and the rivalry of royal headmen.

The principal cleavages in the chiefdom arose from rivalry

among the different royal branches concerning their rights and status and the location of their central villages. The three chiefly branches were not only entitled to provide the chief, but also to participate in his selection. The central villages of all these branches were in the southern part of the chiefdom. The headmen of these villages were associated with the three main Christian churches represented in the chiefdom—the Free Church of Scotland and two African independent churches, Jordan and National—and had played a prominent role in founding congregations in Uyombe. In addition to these three royal branches, there were two others which, although entitled to participate in the chief's selection, were not eligible to provide the chief from among their members. The central villages of both of these branches were in the north; one headman belonged to the Jordan Church and the other to the National Church, but neither had helped to found congregations. Finally there was the Polomombo branch, which had been deprived of the right to select or provide chiefs in the early 1900s. Nonetheless, the Polomombo considered themselves royals, aspired to regain their former status, and continually sought to expand their political influence. They were concentrated in the northeast of the chiefdom, and their central village was Kalinda. Since the turn of this century the principal cleavage within the chiefdom has been that between the Polomombo and the other royal branches.

The Yombe were organized into exogamous, agnatic descent groups which were the basic units of the ancestor cult. The territorial structure was also intimately connected to and supported by the belief in ancestor spirits. The headmen and chief were expected to make annual offerings to their ancestors on behalf of their villages and the chiefdom. The high God, *Leza,* was thought to be distant from the affairs of man. It was the ancestors who were thought to influence daily affairs. The Yombe also believed in witchcraft and sorcery as principal causes of misfortune, and within the context of this framework of beliefs, the ancestors had little control and God, *Leza,* was too remote to interfere. This religious system was particularistic and parochial. It reinforced and reflected the divisions in the society. Christianity introduced new principles of social organization and a new set of assumptions about the world. But it did not displace ancestor worship as the principal religion. For more than 50 years ancestor worship and Christianity have persisted side by side, allowing the Yombe to make use of one or the other or both as the situation dictated. But the Lumpa movement both rejected ancestor worship and condemned the beliefs and practices of other Christian churches, in particular the Free Church, which was the church of the educated elite and the socially aspiring.

IV

The preceding description has attempted not only to set out the principal features of Yombe society, but also to indicate the region in which the Lumpa Church might be expected to find the most enthusiastic following. The northeast was more depressed than the rest of the chiefdom and the social conditions which obtained there would seem to support Roberts' observation that Lenshina's gospel offered more to illiterate villagers and migrant laborers than to Africans with modern skills and some literary education (Roberts 1970: p. 537). The northeast had a history of few and poor schools and a high rate of labor migration. Most men of this area were poorly educated and had been employed in unskilled jobs in the towns, and not as clerks or teachers, or in other similar occupations. While working in the urban areas they could not be considered to be "proletarian intellectuals" in Weber's terms, that is, the intelligentsia of the unprivileged classes (Weber 1965:pp.125-127). Their poor educational background and limited urban and occupational experiences meant that they would rationalize their beliefs and social situation in a different manner than would returning labor migrants who were educated and skilled.

The people of the northeast were highly receptive to new prophecies. Most of the Yombe prophets arose in this region and they acquired an enthusiastic following among both commoners and Polomombo. The Polomombo readily supported new social movements as a means of maintaining and extending their political influence. Thus it is not surprising that the northeast was the center of the Lenshina Movement; in the south there was little interest in it.

Alice Lenshina's reputation as a prophet reached Uyombe in 1955 and among the first to leave for Kasomo, a journey of several days by foot, were the headman of Kalinda and his villagers. The news of their departure spread rapidly and in a few weeks three other headmen and their villagers followed. The Yombe pilgrimage to seek Alice's help in dealing with troubles had begun.

It would appear that many went to Kasomo because of their fear or suspicion of witchcraft, which they suspected was the cause of their misfortunes. In 1964, I talked to the heads of 18 families who claimed to be among the first to make the journey to Kasomo. The reasons they gave for going were as follows: 6 families said that their children were sick, 4 that a child had died recently, 4 that they had dreamed of being bewitched, and 3 that they sought protective medicines against witches. The last was a headman who believed that his villagers were leaving him because they thought he was a witch. He went to Alice to prove that he was not.

On their arrival in Kasomo these first Yombe pilgrims did not find what they expected. Instead of a prophet by herself, they found a church and Alice was its leader. On the morning of their arrival her disciples summoned all newcomers. She stood where they could hear her and asked them if they wanted to join her Church. They agreed and her disciples passed round plates into which each person put a penny. Alice told them that they must obey the rules of the Church and do everything she told them. She said that they must rid themselves of witchcraft and antiwitchcraft medicines since she and God would protect them. Men with more than one wife were instructed to select only one since polygyny was forbidden. The pilgrims were then baptized and became members of her Church. They remained for 4 or more days and underwent instruction; Alice's disciples taught the new members church rules, prayers, and Lumpa Church hymns. As members they were expected to attend her services and listen to her preach. After a week the pilgrims returned to Uyombe.

For many Yombe their stay at Kasomo was more than just spontaneous communitas to use Turner's term (Turner 1969:p.132). It was a profound religious experience which freed them from their former social persona and brought them into a condition of purity. It served as the basis for establishing a spiritual community which was in the world but not subject to it. The giving of a penny was regarded as a symbolic act, cleansing the giver of former sins and enabling him to be reborn into the new spiritual order. As one Yombe preacher put it, "in giving the penny I washed away my sins. I left all things that I did in the past. I raised by right hand and said to Bamama (Alice), 'whatever you tell me to do I will do it . . .' this penny is for God." Membership in the Church not only provided salvation but also brought man closer to God, who Yombe believed would protect them from witchcraft and the forces of evil. The Yombe pilgrims came home with the mission of establishing, through their congregation, spiritual order under the guidance of their prophet Alice.

The central church at Kasomo retained control over its members in a number of ways after they returned home. The Yombe congregation was placed under a Bemba deacon who was expected to make frequent visits. Although he supervised the election of church officers and performed other tasks, neither he nor local church officers had the right to baptize. Accordingly, new converts had to go to Kasomo. Moreover, members were expected to return to Kasomo to help build Alice's church. Through these movements to and fro faith was continually renewed, and the prophet remained the central figure. Alice's following was gradually assuming the form of a permanent and hierarchically arranged religious community. Every local congregation had its own body of officers. The members thus formed an identifiable subgroup bound together by rights and obligations and common ritual, practices, and beliefs. Alice's prophecy had been elaborated into a formal organization but one which demanded the entire allegiance of its members.

                                                                           V

     Eight Lumpa churches were eventually founded in Uyombe drawing their congregations from 19 villages and settlements, all in the northeast. Six of these were established in 1955 and all but one of them eventually moved to Kawulazina, the settlement founded in December 1963 as a reaction to hostilities with U.N.I.P. members and the local government and in anticipation of the new millenium. Of the 16 village headmen and settlement heads who joined the church, 7 were suspended for drinking beer, 4 joined the U.N.I.P., 3 remained members, and 2 died. Of some interest is the fact that at the height of local hostilities between U.N.I.P and the Lumpa, 9 headmen left the Church. Since for them to move to Kawulazina entailed the loss of their prestigious posts it is not surprising that the 3 headmen who did move were also Church officers, 2 being preachers and 1 a judge.
     The Bemba deacon, who made frequent visits to Uyombe, usually stayed for a month or so. He supervised the founding of churches and the election of preachers, preached and evangelized, and collected information on local church problems. Each church had its own officers, choir, and congregation. The officers were the preachers, the judges, and the choirmaster.
     The preachers, who were the most important officers, were selected from the congregation. The post was open to both men and

women, and in theory there should have been 4 for each church; in fact, some churches had more and some less. Only the deacon could organize the election of a preacher. After spending some time with a congregation, he would assemble its members, ask those who wanted to be preachers to stand, and call for a show of hands. The election then had to be approved by Alice at Kasomo. On the deacon's next visit he would announce the new preachers. Most of those selected had been among the first to join the church in Kasomo. The eight Yombe churches had 29 preachers, 23 men, and 7 women. Of the 23 men only 1 had completed standard VI (8 years of schooling). Their average level of schooling was standard II (or 4 years of schooling). Although I could get little information on this point, it would seem that the number of preachers was related to the size of the congregation.

The preachers had many duties but here I intend to give only a few. They supervised church affairs and represented their congregation in its dealings with other Christian churches, local government, and U.N.I.P. They administered the sacraments of marriage and burial, but they could not baptize. There was no communion since the symbolic act of consuming the blood and flesh of Christ was regarded as an ancestor rite. In each church the preachers organized revival meetings and played host to the seven other congregations. In the final phases of Lumpa activity, these meetings often led to fights with non-Lumpa members. After these incidents, the local authority, the Native Administration, would summon the leaders of both sides, but Lumpa members refused to appear. The fights became more frequent as the struggle for Zambian independence intensified.

The preachers were intermediaries between their congregations and Alice. All matters which they considered beyond their competence were referred to Kasomo. These might concern the founding of new branches, but most frequently they involved such cases as breaches of church rules.

In general, two elements governed the selection, duties and the decisions of the preachers. There was the personal element of the prophet which permeated the fabric of the Church. Alice had to approve his selection, and her personal representative, the deacon, supervised the performance of his duties. She made decisions which the preacher was supposed to carry out. His allegiance was to her, not to an office. The second element was an impersonal one, the normative order, consisting of the rules governing the recruitment of the preacher, the performance of his duties, and the spheres in which he could take decisions. These two elements, the personal and the normative, intermeshed and helped to define the emerging structure of the Church. The preachers and other officers held allegiance to the prophet but they were also loyal to the Church.

Each church was supposed to have two judges. This post was also open to both men and women, and election to it was supervised by the preachers and required neither the presence of the deacon nor Alice's confirmation. The eight churches had only ten judges, 7 men and 3 women. Their primary duty was to deal with breaches of Church rules. Every member was responsible for reporting infractions to the preachers, who in turn informed the judges. If the offense was a minor one such as cursing, the offender was summoned by the judges and told to correct his ways. But in case of a serious offense, such as drinking beer or smoking in the church area, the offender would be suspended from church membership, though not from church attendance. The judges made the decision, but it was the preachers who informed the offender of it. The offender was expected to attend services, and both in and out of church his conduct was closely observed by church members. Once the period of suspension was over he could apply to the preachers for readmission as a full member of the congregation. In the Lumpa Church suspension was taken more seriously than it was by members of other churches, since it was thought to place members in a dangerous position. They entered that amorphous zone between sacred and profane worlds and thus were more vulnerable to the evil forces of Satan such as witchcraft.

In its later phases, the Lumpa Church forbade members to have any cases heard by secular authorities. The Church itself settled disputes, and if members were summoned before government authorities or the Native Administration court in Muyombe, the capital of the chiefdom, they refused to appear.

Under the leadership of its preachers and judges, the Yombe Lumpa Church became a tightly knit theocratic community, demanding the complete allegiance of its members and dominating their lives. By 1962, members of the Church were refusing to obey the laws of the chiefdom and even to meet their obligations to kinsmen, friends, and neighbors. They also refused to join U.N.I.P. or in any other way support it. The final step was for the Church to build its own settlement.

During the 1963 national elections in Zambia the number of violent clashes between U.N.I.P. and the Lumpa increased. In the context of this strife-ridden situation, the Yombe Lumpa preachers

said that they had received a message from Alice that the end of the
world was rapidly approaching, and that members should leave their
villages and their worldly goods and found a new settlement, Kawulazina, in the northeastern tip of Uyombe, some 30 miles from
Muyombe. Kawulazina was an unauthorized settlement, and in January 1964 the District Commissioner (D.C.) of Isoka and local government and U.N.I.P. officers went there to order the Lumpa to return
to their villages. For Lumpa, Kawulazina was sacred and any one
who entered it was expected to abide by Church rules. A member of
the D.C.'s party made the mistake of lighting a cigarette, and the
D.C. and those with him were chased from the settlement by Lumpa
armed with a variety of lethal weapons. This incident brought home
to the authorities the serious nature of the situation. Although Rotberg described the Lumpa as anti-European and anticolonial (1961:p.
75), in 1964 the Church was opposed to any external authority
whatever. Similar incidents were occurring throughout the Northern
and Eastern Provinces. In July 1964, there was widespread fighting
in both Provinces in which a large number of people were killed. During this conflict the Yombe Lumpa, consisting of 255 persons, were
arrested and imprisoned at Isoka District headquarters. While in
detention they retained the structure of their Church. My principal
contact with them was in the Isoka detention camp and after their
release in Uyombe.

VI

The reformist orientation of the Lumpa Church is apparent in
the area of beliefs, the way in which it rationalized the world in
Christian terms, and the extent to which its religious beliefs were distinct from ancestor worship. Most preachers and judges condemned
the Free Church for failing to adhere to its own fundamentalist principles. They thought it had allowed Satan to gain control to such an
extent that God had had to enter into the everyday affairs of man by
sending Alice Lenshina who represented the second appearance of
Christ.

Among the Yombe Lumpa there was a sense of religious im-
mediacy and validity in their beliefs that was not found in other
Christian churches. God and Satan, the spirits of their religion, were
thought to be near to man, contending for his soul and his actions.
God and Satan were thought to be concerned with, and part of, the
world as a whole but, as omnipresent spirits, they were near to man.

They used their spiritual powers to influence the course of events, vying with each other for men's souls. The ancestors, *viwanda,* who had formerly been thought to be concerned with the everyday events, were excluded from this drama. For adherents of the traditional religion they were the source of good and evil fortune and buttressed traditional institutions and morality. But they were not part of the Lumpa inventory of spirits. In a manner of speaking, the universal had displaced the particular. Good and evil fortune ceased to be related to lesser, local spirits and were attributed to God or Satan. Since ancestor spirits had been rejected, they could no longer serve to explain or predict local events, nor could they attempt to control such events. The Lumpa considered that Jesus Christ was the son of God, the intermediary spirit standing between man and God. Jesus was the spirit that was thought to inhabit Alice Mulenga.

The Lumpa viewed God as the creator of all things. He was the supreme benevolent spirit protecting and providing for man. Satan had been created by God as a good spirit, but he had turned against Him and sought to usurp His place. Satan was driven from heaven and resided on earth, tempting man away from the path of God. He was the source of evil, and it was from him that witches were thought to derive their powers to harm man. The baptismal rites of the Lumpa Church not only purified man, but also exorcised evil, including witchcraft. Although the Lumpa did not reject the belief in witchcraft, they viewed their Church membership and their hymns and prayers as safeguards against it. Their techniques of approaching God were highly developed, providing them with immediate protection against the evil of Satan. They believed that Satan was attempting to take over the world and that those who refused to join the Lumpa Church, were not only prone to evil but were part of Satan's scheme. For the Lumpa, their church was the only source of salvation, of security from the evil forces that were rapidly gaining control over Uyombe, Zambia, and the world. God had sent his son Jesus to save man, and in 1953 He sent Alice Mulenga.

Within the general schema of Yombe ancestor worship and Christianity, it was the heads of social groups who were expected to pray to spirits. The heads of ancestor cults prayed to the ancestors and the heads of churches prayed to Jesus. Yombe Christians believed that Jesus delivered prayers to his Father. God was far from man and should not be prayed to directly. The Lumpa also considered Jesus an intermediary between man and God, but it was not to Him that Lumpa turned in situations of trouble, rites of passage, or before undertaking a task; Jesus could not protect them against

Satan. When confronted with troubles they prayed directly to God, and ritual practitioners were not an integral part of their beliefs.

For Lumpa, Alice's appearance was the second coming of Christ, but she did not possess the same attributes of spirit. Her powers and message were thought to come from God. God spoke to her but she was not as Jesus, a spirit. She was not the recipient of prayers, although the rules which she laid down and her pronouncements were believed to be from God. Persons who did not belong to her Church were excluded from the ranks of the saved and had accepted the ways of Satan. Salvation was only possible through joining the Lumpa Church, following its precepts, and obeying the words of Alice. Because the Lumpa were unable to convert the world to their religion, their only recourse was to withdraw from it. Thus, they founded a sacred community, to await God's retribution on the non-believers and the beginning of the millenium in which they, as God's chosen people, would rule the earth.

From this brief description of Lumpa beliefs it should be apparent that the traditional belief in ancestor worship was entirely rejected. Instead, the Lumpa had returned to a simple form of Christianity in which the events of the world and human actions were explained in terms of God and Satan, the forces of good and evil. The movement was reformist, an attempt on the part of a poorly educated section of Yombe society to come to grips with their position in a rapidly changing world by reestablishing the fundamentalist teachings of early mission Christianity. They removed themselves from the contemporary world and sought security in a new society based upon Christian principles.

VII

Once the Lumpa had been defeated and imprisoned there remained the major task of reintegrating them into Zambian society. The central government decided to return them to their original chiefdoms, leaving much of the responsibility of resettling them to the Native Administrations of the District.

In Uyombe the local government formed the Lenshina Resettlement Committee (LRC) to supervise the return and settlement of the 255 Lumpa. This committee consisted of local government and U.N.I.P. officers and other men who were well educated by rural Zambian standards. Most had completed at least 8 years of schooling and, while working outside of Uyombe, had been employed as clerks and teachers. They were part of the intelligentsia of the African rural elite. They were either members of or attended the Free Church. They represented that section of Yombe society which sought to bring about change through practical political means and not on the basis of religious belief.

The main tasks of the committe were to resettle the Lumpa and to make sure that they did not pursue their fatih; the Lumpa Church was banned by government. The committee divided the detainees into five groups based upon the extent of their commitment to the Church. The hard core Lumpa followers formed the last group to be returned to the chiefdom. The leaders of the Church were assigned to villages whose headmen were noted for their strength of character and for their efficiency in carrying out the policies of local government. Although most Lumpa abided by the ban placed on worship, about 5% refused to accept the prohibition on engaging in Lumpa religious practices. This group, most of whom were close agnates, fled to Zaire where the Lumpa had founded a community.

The manner in which returned Lumpa sought to reintegrate themselves into Yombe society reveals some of the core elements of Yombe ideology. Through their acts Lumpa had rejected Yombe society in a most fundamental way. They had placed themselves outside society and community and were thus viewed by the Yombe as presenting an imminent danger to the social order and to the constituent elements of the dominant ideological field of their society. The Lumpa had rejected ideological premises which buttressed and rationalized social "reality."

Perhaps the most vivid and pronounced display of Yombe emotions toward the Lumpa occurred when they were brought from their settlement to Muyombe. The road was lined with onlookers, and along with extensive jeering and cries of "murderers"—the Yombe Lumpa had in fact killed no one—the most frequent exclamation was that of "mad dogs." This term was also the primary one used by the rehabilitation committee toward the groups of returning detainees. For the Yombe, the dog is an important domestic animal, noted for loyalty, obedience, and respect for its master. The domesticated dog is of society whereas a dog that has gone mad is not only not of society, but has become something even more threatening than a creature of the wild. A mad dog represents great danger and should be killed on the spot. The Lumpa were thought to be of the same order of abomination, and if it had not been for the intervention of government troops, they would have been harmed.

The Lumpa had consciously rejected the assumptions basic to

the dominant ideological field in which the governing principles of Yombe kinship and citizenship were embodied. They accepted neither ancestor worship nor agnatic kinship and denied the continuity of blood as the essential substance for the social recognition of "real" kinship (Barnett 1978:p.276). They rejected the Chief, the royal clan, and all other secular authority and removed themselves into the bush. They were a community apart, one whose residents had relinquished all rights as kinsmen, friends, and citizens. They were "mad dogs," living in and from the bush "without salt," as several Yombe put it to me.

Although the returning Yombe Lumpa did not view either themselves or their church in these terms, they did recognize the steps which they needed to take in order to reintegrate themselves into Yombe society. The first step was to acknowledge the ancestor cult by claiming ancestor visitation in dreams, and then to renew membership in the ancestor cult by making sacrifices to the ancestors. Acknowledgment of the ancestor cult also served to reintegrate the Lumpa into their agnatic descent groups. The second step necessary for the returning of Lumpa was to acknowledge publicly the authority of the chief. In some instances this was done inconspicuously in front of the village headman and his advisors, but some Lumpa acknowledged the chief dramatically by prostrating themselves before him and exclaiming his praises. The third step was to seek membership of the Free Church or one of the more prominent independent churches, Jordan or National. The final step was to apply to U.N.I.P. for membership. Through these various steps an individual could reestablish his social persona not only as kinsmen and citizen but also as a reputable Christian and party member. He had demonstrated his acceptance of local and national institutions and his subordinate position within them.

VIII

In this chapter I have attempted not only to describe the social conditions which were conducive to the emergence of a new Christian movement but also to characterize the religious features of the movement. Turner's notion of normative communitas seems to apply to the position of the Lumpa Church in Yombe society (Turner 1969:p.131). The Church emerged from a religious experience, a "happening" as it were, among a people from a politically and economically depressed area of Zambia. The political leaders of the

northeastern area of Uyombe were the Polomombo who were excluded from the mainstream of the political process of the chiefdom
and the people of the area thus had minimal say in chiefdom affairs.
Historically, the people of this area were prone to accept new prophecies and so, when they heard of Alice, many of them made the
arduous trek to Kasomo. For many, their experience at Kasomo was
more than a "happening" in that it formed the basis of religious conversion and for developing a spiritual community. To paraphrase
Turner, the existential communitas was organized into a perduring
social grouping (1969:p.131); one which was based upon the principles of early mission teachings and one which was reformist in its
character and orientation.

Yombe society demonstrates a high level of functional integration in that its institutions are intimately interrelated and interde-
pendent. Ancestor worship, which underpinned the moral order and
buttressed political authority, was not displaced by either the Free
Church or the African independent churches, Jordan and National.
Ancestor worship and Christianity persisted side by side, providing
the Yombe with a number of exclusive religious options as well as
different bases upon which to justify or rationalize their choices,
decisions, and actions. The Yombe allowed for situational ambiguity
and selection related to the nature of the social context. The Lumpa
could not accept this type of ambiguity. They entirely rejected
ancestor worship and the belief in ancestors and opposed other
Christian churches. The Lumpa Church and its members would not,
and perhaps could not, be integrated into Yombe society. It emerged
as the antithesis to established religious forms and became a self-
contained religious community, a foreign element within the fabric
of Yombe society, whose members held allegiance to a Bemba
prophet and a church that governed their lives. The Lumpa felt that
they were not responsible to the Yombe Chief or to their fellow
Yombe, but only to Lumpa. Thus, their Church formed the basis of
an antistructure which sought to subvert the existing social order and
to replace it with a new one.

During the 1950s Yombe society, with the rest of Zambia, was
undergoing rapid social change. The traditional belief system, which
was particularistic and parochial, could not provide an explanation of
this order of change, nor could it expand its precepts to encompass a
multiethnic religious movement which disregarded all forms of social
boundaries and brought its adherents into a state of "normative
communitas."

In many respects the traditional religion of the Yombe fits

Horton's characterization of a "typical traditional cosmology" based
upon a two-tiered system of ideas relating to the scale of the community and the domain of spirits (Horton 1971:p.101). In this
schema the supreme being is distant and concerned with the world as
a whole, the macrocosm, but not with the ordinary, everyday events
of the local community, the microcosm. Few events are attributed
to the agency of the supreme being who is not concerned with
human morality. The means of approaching him are poorly developed. The lesser spirits are in charge of the local community and
most events, fortunate or unfortunate, are attributed to their agency.
Not only are they directly involved in human affairs, but they also
reinforce morality. Horton considers that the "microcosm is to a
considerable extent insulated from the macrocosm of the wider
world [1971: p. 101]." Social change may, however, lead to a collapse
in the boundaries and the displacement (or replacement) of lesser
spirits by the supreme being.

Horton's formulation may at first seem inappropriate to the
Yombe case. After all, for more than 50 years the Yombe have been
involved in labor migration and have had extensive experience with
towns, the centers of social change, but they have still retained their
ancestor cults. Moreover, they had accepted Christianity, even
though the Christian churches had entered along the lines of political
cleavages. But viewed from another perspective, change within
Uyombe was, until the 1950s, a gradual, incremental process. For
most of the colonial period the boundaries of the society were maintained intact, as was the authority of the Native Authority, the chief.
Christianity, as it was practiced by the Free Church and the National
and Jordan Churches, did not in practice interfere with ancestor worship, whereas the Lumpa specifically rejected belief in the power of
ancestors and attributed evil and troubles to Satan. The uncertainties
of a rapidly changing world could be explained in terms of the
struggle being waged between God and Satan.

My account of the rise and fall of the Lumpa Church in
Uyombe may help to throw further light upon the more general issue
of the nature of the relationship between political and religious excitement—that is, whether political and religious enthusiasms or
activity occur together, or whether the one rises as the other sub-
sides. Both Hobsbawm and Thompson have concerned themselves
with this issue. Hobsbawm has made the point that there is a "marked parallelism" between religious and political movements (Hobsbawm 1959: p. 130) whereas Thompson discussing the eighteenth- to
nineteenth-century England, appears to feel that waves of politics

and religious activity followed one after the other. He states that "it is possible that religious revivalism took over just at the point where 'political' or temporal aspirations met with defeat [Thompson 1974: p. 389]."

Africanists such as Balandier (1965:pp. 54-55), Hodgkin (1956: pp.93-115), Rotberg (1961:p.75), and Sundkler (1961) viewed African prophetic movement as safety valves or proto political movements for anticolonial expressions. It was commonly thought that with the rise of African political parties and the end of colonial rule, African prophetic movements would wane. However, in the Northern Province of Zambia the successful growth of the Lumpa Church coincided with that of U.N.I.P. Both in their early phases were anticolonial and sought the dominance of Africans. But while U.N.I.P. retained its secular goals of bringing about an independent Zambia, the Lumpa turned against secular authority, European or African, and sought spiritual hegemony in a projected chiliastic holocaust in which they would survive supreme. The promise was apparently sufficiently appealing to entrance a large number of adherents, many of whom died fighting government troops in the belief that they would find life in death. "Jericho" and "Hallelujah" were believed to be the key to a successful transition and, thus, many died shouting either "Jericho" or "Hallelujah."

The crucial point in appraising the relationship betwen the growth of U.N.I.P. and that of the Lumpa Church lies, it seems to me, in examining the sources of their support. My purpose at this point is not to examine individual incidence of choice but to explore the nature of the segment of the population to which the Lumpa appealed. Those who joined and remained in the movement consisted primarily of the less educated and poorer rungs of the peasantry. They were for the most part the former laboring poor of the towns, mines, and plantations of east, central, and southern Africa, who returned home to cultivate land in villages distant from the commercial center of the chiefdom Muyombe. Put differently, they had formed the lower rungs of the urban proletariat while abroad as labor migrants and, on their return home, they constituted that segment of the peasantry which was least prosperous in terms of cash, education, and prospects, whereas U.N.I.P. recruited many of its adherents from the better educated and somewhat more affluent segments of Yombe society. In both their rural and urban experiences the Lumpa had occupied a subordinate position. The fact that they were the poor peasants of the countryside and were the former laboring poor of the urban centers provided them with, in Giddens' terms, "class awareness" but not class consciousness (Giddens 1974:p.111). It was this diffuse awareness of themselves as an oppressed segment of society which placed them firmly in the lower ranks of the "common people" (Hobsbawm 1972:p.10). It was also this awareness of their condition which, in my opinion, made them receptive to a fundamentalist, Christian movement which stressed egalitarian, other worldliness, and those values or properties which Turner attributes to conditions of spontaneous and normative communitas (Turner 1974: p.169). The religion of the Lumpa was an inversion of social reality. Its primitive chiliastic presumptions promised that the meek would inherit the earth. It was a reformist movement which sought to restore fundamental Christian (Free Church) values. Espousing the beliefs of the Lumpa Church, rather than devoting energies to U.N.I.P., hindered the development of class consciousness as a radical mobilizing force. The church's opposition was to the "traditional" as well as contemporary elements of Yombe society. It was not a revitalistic movement, but one which sought to reestablish the fundamentalist teachings of the Free Church of Scotland. The Lumpa believed that this church was the last refuge of man. Security, certainty, protection from evil, and of course, salvation, were within the church. That which could not be reformed, the world outside the community of the select, should and would be destroyed by God, or so the Lumpa believed.

ACKNOWLEDGMENTS

I owe a debt of thanks to Merran Fraenkel who insisted that I collect detailed material on Lumpa returnees. I am also indebted to Lucy Mair and Alison Murray for their critical comments and assistance in retaining the academic focus of the article.

REFERENCES

Balandier, G. "Messianism and Nationalism in Black Africa" in Van Den Berghe (Ed.) *Africa.* Chandler Publishing Co., 1965.

Balandier, G. "The Colonial Situation" in M. Wallerstein (Ed.) *Social Change.* New York: John Wiley and Sons, 1966.

Barber, W. J. *The Economy of British Central Africa.* London: Oxford University Press, 1961.

Barnett, S. "Identity Choice and Caste Ideology in Contemporary South India" in J. Dolgin, D. Kemnitzer and D. Schneider (Eds.) *Symbolic Anthropology.* New York: Columbia University Press, 1978.

Bond, G. "Kinship and Conflict in a Yombe Village" *Africa,* Vol. XLII, No. IV, Oct., 1972.

Bond, G. *The Politics of Change in a Zambian Community.* Chicago: Chicago University Press, 1976.

Giddens, A. *The Class Structure of the Advanced Societies.* London: Hutchinson and Co., 1973.

Hobsbawm, E. J. "Class Consciousness in History" in Istvan Meszaros (Ed.) *Aspects of History and Class Consciousness.* New York: Herder and Herder, 1972.

Hobsbawm, E. J. *Primitive Rebels.* New York: W. W. Norton and Company, 1959.

Hodgkin, T. *Nationalism in Colonial Africa.* London: Frederick Muller, 1956.

Horton, R. "African Conversion" *Africa,* Vol. XLI, No. 2, April, 1971.

Jules-Rosette, B. *African Apostles.* Ithaca: Cornell University Press, 1975.

Marx, K. *The Eighteenth Brumaire of Louis Bonaparte.* New York: International Publishers, 1975.

Oger, L. "Le Mouvement Lenshina en Rhodesie du Nord" in *Eglise Vivante,* Vol. XIV, Paris, 1962.

Report of the Commission of Enquiry into the Former Lumpa Church, Lusaka, 1965.

Roberts, A. "The Lumpa Church of Alice Lenshina" in R. I. Rotberg and A. A. Mazrui *Protest and Power in Black Africa.* New York: Oxford Press, 1970.

Rotberg, R. I. "The Lenshina Movement of Northern Rhodesia" *The Rhodes-Livingston Journal,* XXIX, 1961.

Sundkler, B. G. *Bantu Prophets in South Africa.* Oxford University Press, 1961.

Taylor, J. and Lehmann, D. A. *Christians of the Copperbelt.* London: S.C.M. Press, 1961.

Thompson, E. P. *The Making of the English Working Class.* New York: Vintage Books, 1963.

Turner, V. W. *The Ritual Process.* Chicago: Aldine, 1969.

Turner, V. W. *Dramas, Fields and Metaphors.* Ithaca: Cornell University Press, 1974.

Weber, M. *The Sociology of Religion.* London: Methuen and Co., 1965.

DISCUSSION

The chapters contained in this volume present a variety of African Christian Churches that are viewed by the authors as manifestations of indigenous religious initiative, continuous with local religious history. This approach implies that there are specifically African versions of Christianity as varied in form and content as the configuration of circumstances that sparked their creation, which are, however, similar in many fundamental ways and share common differences from the brands of Christianity originally offered by European missionaries. A fundamental methodological and theoretical consequence of this approach is that these religious movements are not viewed as foreign institutions grafted onto an African cultural base, but rather as African social forms that are part of and merge into the indigenous historical process. In all cases, the African populations embraced certain elements of the missionaries' Christianity, rejected other elements, and remolded still others to create the new and unique syntheses that constitute African Christianity in all of its myriad varieties. This comparative ethnography demonstrates some of the kinds of forms Christianity has taken in Africa and the kinds of roles it has played in various African contexts.

From the perspective of the sociology of religion, Christian movements in Africa offer an opportunity to study the genesis of religious beliefs, practices, and organizations and to consider the social conditions and historical circumstances in which they arose. The Harrist, Apostolo, and Lumpa movements as well as the Church of the Messiah were all founded by Africans in the twentieth century, and although the African Methodist Episcopal (A.M.E.) Church did not originate in Africa, it was African initiative that resulted in its emergence in Zambia. A central theme in the articles concerns the process of change within indigenous societies and changes in the relationships between the traditional and modern sectors of the larger society.

II

Change is the context within which the nature of these religious movements must be assessed. The narrow, particularistic features of indigenous, localized and basically agrarian religions could not provide the basis for dealing with the new social systems developing during the period of colonial rule. The movements were attempts to introduce new modes of conceptualizing reality in order to cope with contemporary concerns. Local belief systems were frequently ill suited for the variety of new conditions and expectations that were most apparent in the modern setting but which also penetrated and affected the very fabric of rural societies. Christianity, with its more universal set of principles, expanded the range of explanatory potential.

Within the context of the urban-industrial centers of Africa, the individual's relation to the means of production and to property, as well as his perception of himself and his relationships to others, have undergone changes. In pre-colonial rural societies, relationships based upon status were a pervasive feature; an individual's rights in basic resources were in large part a function of his position in an ascriptive system of allocations. But in the contemporary urban centers, contract is the more pervasive basis of social relationships, especially in those spheres of human activity involving subsistence and property relations. The pervasiveness of contractual arrangements not only weakens the control of traditional groups over their members but also provides the individual with a degree of freedom. Yet this freedom is in part an illusion, since the economic system is based primarily on contractual agreements that subordinate him to the demands and fluctuations of a market system in which his human worth and social position may be measured in monetary terms. From another perspective, the movement from status to contract may be seen as part of the system of urban social stratification based upon class.

This formulation suggests a relation between the functions of new religious movements and the changing bases for social relationships in contemporary African societies. Although most of the religious movements discussed were rooted in the underprivileged classes, it is inappropriate to describe them as religions of the oppressed. The congregations of these movements were related to the systems of social stratification in different ways, and their teachings, beliefs, and practices reflected these differences. The A.M.E. Church and the Church of the Messiah both emphasized individualism and the contractual nature of urban life. They reinforced the demands of the urban class system and provided the context for acquiring values and norms suitable for movement within it. Religious beliefs and practices were made appropriate to the mundane circumstances of everyday life. There was not a rejection of the secular world but an acceptance of it. The A.M.E. Church had a narrow vision of its religious hegemony over its members and did not intrude into their everyday affairs.

The Church of the Messiah had a more inclusive view of its purpose and catered to the troubles and misfortunes of its members; healing, for example, was an important dimension of the church. The Church was concerned not only with contract but also with the troubles that stemmed from persons as members of groups formulated on ascriptive principles. Put differently, the Church of the Messiah mediated the basic contradictions that were to be found in the demands of domestic life based on status and rooted in kinship and those of public life based upon contract and rooted in achievement within the modern economic and commercial sector of Labadi.

In contrast to these two urban churches the Lumpa church represents a different type of reaction to the growing class system of urban society. The Lumpa Church attempted to reconstitute the totality of the individual into a single religious persona. The individual was made subordinate within the confines of a social community in which only relationships of status were recognized. So reconstituted, the Lumpa were the select, superior to all nonmembers. This view of themselves was, however, a reversal of their actual position in society. Social subordination was replaced by spiritual superordination.

The contrast between the A.M.E. and the Church of the Messiah, on the one hand, and the Lumpa, on the other, reveals another feature of these Christian movements. It is common to stress the ethnic, linguistic, and cultural diversity of church members. The heterogeneity of the membership is often taken as an indication of the wide appeal of these churches as an indication of growing cultural integration along religious lines. There is, however, another possibility. Although the appeal may be to culturally diverse populations, the membership may be predominantly from one particular stratum of society. Put differently, the apparent cultural homogenization of African populations in religious organizations may in fact be a statement of growing trends of social stratification based upon a class system. Congregations may increasingly reflect the class structure. Thus, cultural and ethnic heterogeneity may be replaced by class homogeneity within the context of religious movements.

The period during which African Christian movements arose was characterized not only by rapid social transformation but also by rising nationalist sentiments. The political and social degradation of being colonized constituted the context in which an expression of African self-esteem was meaningful. It is significant that none of the movements analyzed here actually engaged, as organizations, in the struggle for political power. But each church clearly had an "African" character. This feature suggests a positive relationship between African Christian movements and a broader African nationalism, a nationalism not limited to political and economic concerns but one which encompasses religious and cultural foci. These movements indicate the formation of an African consciousness which accepts the intrinsic value of things African and naturalizes them within the Christian tradition. This process of naturalization is a distinctive feature of these movements and accounts for much of this popular appeal.

III

Just as the data presented suggest a more sophisticated analysis of the relationship between African Christianity and a sense of nationalism that goes beyond the purely political, they also call into question the tendency to suggest a simple correlation between urbanization and the development of such movements. Although most African Christian movements have developed in urban or peri-urban areas, and clearly reflect the concerns of such areas, neither the rural dimension of many movements nor the emphasis on issues entirely unrelated to urbanization characteristic of others can be ignored.

The Lumpa Church was basically a rural movement and although the headquarters of the Apostolo and A.M.E. Churches were urban, they too had a number of rural congregations. Walker addressed this issue specifically in describing the relationship between the religious concerns and activities of a movement and its sociogeographic location. Movements located in more remote areas tend to focus on the traditional concerns of healing and witchcraft eradication, whereas those located closer to urban areas tend to have a broader spectrum of concerns. The issues of healing and witchcraft are, however, often present in the urban movements and, in many instances, such as in the Church of the Messiah, may be reinterpreted in terms of the concerns of modern urban life.

IV

African Christian movements spread as a result of the evangelical work of Africans. For the Lumpa, Apostolo, and Church of the Messiah, regulating growth was a constant problem. Two factors seem to be of prime importance in analyzing how African Christian movements spread. They are: (*a*) the presence or absence of a theological authority; (*b*) the presence or absence of an organizational authority. ity.

The A.M.E. Church did not experience problems in regulating growth or in establishing sources of legitimate authority since it was an older institution with regularized procedures. However, the Harrist, Apostolo, and Lumpa were all religious movements in which the organizational structure was still being worked out. In these cases much seems to depend upon the prophet's or founder's initial intent as well as on the style of propagation. The Lumpa Church was in an earlier phase of development, and authority was derived directly from the person of the prophetess. Only Alice Lenshina had the spiritual power to perform the critical rite of baptism, and local congregations could only be established with her personal approval. Consequently, the movement and its expansion remained under the direction of the prophetess.

The Harrist and Apostolo movements, by contrast, differ in both their degree of centralization and their style of propagation. The crucial difference lay in the intent of the prophets and in the existence or not of a single source of spiritual authority. Harris' intention was not to be the center of a religious institution, but rather to inspire a religious revolution. He was the bringer of a message, not the founder of a church. Various people were therefore able to found diverse movements in his name based only on the broad outlines of his message. John Maranke's intent, on the contrary, was to found a movement based on his spiritual revelations which provided the ultimate source of orthodoxy and orthopraxy. Consequently, subsequent church leaders confronted the difficult task of maintaining control over distant congregations and of enforcing religious orthodoxy because individual congregations tended to adjust beliefs and practices to local customs.

Adopting an analytical framework based on the preceding factors helps clarify certain of the terminology used with regard to the spread of these movements. "Schism," "proliferation," "growth" are all terms used to refer to the spread of the movements. It is the value preferences which usually determine the term that is employed. "Schism" is bad or negative, while "growth" is good and positive.

An analytical framework based on the preceding factors clarifies the processes involved in the spread of a movement and eliminates many of the value-laden interpretations. The chapters in this volume suggest that when the theological authority is alive and present, he or she also constitutes the organizational authority. As in the case of the Lumpa, spread of the movement is considered "growth" because it occurs with the requisite legitimation. By definition there can be no "schism" because an illegitimate offshoot of the movement would cease to be part of the movement.

When the theological authority is absent but there is an organizational authority, as with Apostolo, breakaways are considered "schisms" because they threaten the central organization. Where both the theological and organizational authority are absent, as in Harrist Churches, spread can be seen as "proliferation."

V

African Christian churches developing in the context of social change acted as adaptive institutions. Unlike traditional religious organizations, many of the new churches, particularly those in rapidly urbanizing areas, were voluntary associations that constituted partial substitutes for kin-based relationships and functioned as instruments for coping with a changing social scene. The urban churches provided mutual aid and a sense of belonging and were agencies of social control and mechanisms for achieving status, prestige, and leadership in terms of modern criteria.

Johnson's analysis explicitly delineates some aspects of the

A.M.E. Church's role as a voluntary association. Mullings also illustrates how the Church of the Messiah assumes the attributes of a voluntary association. Curiously, perhaps because it is the least apparent, the Lumpa church also embodies the characteristics of a voluntary association to a high degree. The rejection of all authority, including customary obligations to kin and neighbors, represents the adoption of radically new values and norms by Lumpa followers. The demand for full spiritual commitment to Alice constituted the basis for exercising social control and for the dispensing of mutual aid.

An important aspect in the relationship of these African Christian churches to other elements of indigenous culture lies in the construction of new belief systems. These new belief systems, however, support the idea of a continuity between the "traditional" and the "modern" world views, as established beliefs are interpreted in contemporary terms and customary concepts evolve into a modern doctrine. Systems of belief symbolize and reflect social reality and also provide the framework for interpreting it. Social reality throughout most of Africa includes both customary and recently acquired features. Urbanism for example is a contemporary aspect of social reality for most Africans, whereas fear of witchcraft is a perennial aspect. The world view and belief system of most modern Africans therefore must constitute a means of interpreting a social reality which is composed of well-established as well as recently developed features.

African Christian churches incorporate beliefs and practices from indigenous culture into their world views and thereby maintain relevance to the complex social reality of their constituency. The Lumpa Church, for instance, while discarding ancestor worship and disavowing the legitimacy of all customary religious authority, nevertheless protected its members from witchcraft and sorcery. For the Lumpa, witchcraft and sorcery were real forces of evil that had to be dealt with, and the church's belief system explained and helped its members cope with this dimension of social reality.

The African movements described here fulfilled this function for their members in different ways. The Lumpa, Apostolo, Church of the Messiah, and Harrist Churches incorporated into their Christian doctrine new interpretations and new ways of coping with witchcraft. The A.M.E. Church did not address the issue in its formal doctrine yet tolerated its members' continued belief in witchcraft and their recourse to specialists in time of need. The Harrists have added the prohibition of witchcraft to the Ten Commandments and consider it to be the most significant one. The Apostolo Church the language of witchcraft is used to explain disputes over authority.

VII

These ethnographic studies have theoretical and methodological implications as well as suggestions for future research areas in the study of African Christian movements. In regard to theory, the wide variety of belief systems and organizational structures represented here supports the search for lower level theory. The differences between these movements far exceed their similarities—the major common elements being that they are all Christian and that they have emerged during a period of intense social change within African societies. In regard to doctrine, ritual, geography, leadership, mode of evolution, method of incorporating customary beliefs, and the like, there are significant differences. Broad generalizations are therefore clearly unsuitable. Many current researchers seek "middle range" theory. But lower level theory or a different kind of generalization may be required lest we seek unifying elements where they do not exist and fail to take cognizance of the distinctive features and dynamics characteristic of each particular movement.

One specific theoretical notion implied in each of the articles is that African Christian movements should be understood as part of the natural process of religious change in Africa. Scholars, such as H. W. Turner (1967), Wishlade (1965), and Sundkler (1961), who emphasize the "syncretic" character of African Christian movements, have unwittingly misphrased the major issue, thus pointing us in a direction that is not fruitful. They have sought to find the "cause" for the emergence of the movements and have viewed them as reactions to missionizing or to the European presence. The cause of change cannot be isolated. Rather scholars must explore the factors that influence the speed and direction of change. Much of the literature seems to ignore this point. Some writers, for instance, suggest that the need for a belief system to explain, predict, and control space-time events constitutes the "causal" motivation for the construction of new religions. Certainly many churches have this attribute, but can one justify seeing a causal relationship? Similarly, researchers who find "political" or "psychological" causes miss the mark slightly. One must recognize that religion in Africa is constantly evolving and that African Christian movements are contemporary expressions of religious change. Barrett (1968) and Mbiti (1969) have led in this direction by emphasizing that the new religions are seeking to "indigenize" Christianity. Even this formulation, however, focuses attention on the foreign origin of the theological framework rather than upon the African origins of the new institutions and belief systems.

This collection has attempted to place African Christianity within the context of African religious life and to demonstrate its innovative features in reformulating experience. Africa has undergone rapid change, so also have its religious beliefs and practices. New syntheses, based upon this changing reality, are continually emerging. Tension is always present between the precepts of religious life and the demands of everday life. This tension provides for a continuing dialectic, a constant state of transformation and adaptation and yet for continuity. It is African Christianity which in many parts of Africa provides for that continuity which shapes religious experience and places demands in its turn on everyday life.

REFERENCES

Barrett, D.B. *Schism and Renewal in Africa.* Nairobi: Oxford University Press, 1968.
Geertz, C. "Religion as a Cultural System"   *Anthropological Approaches to the Study of Religion.* M. Banton (ed.), London: Tavistock, 1966.
Goody, J. "Religion and Ritual: The Definitional Problem"   *British Journal of Sociology* 12 (2), 1961.
Horton, R. "A Definition of Religion and its Uses"   *Journal of the Royal Anthropological Institute* 90 (2), July-December, 1960.
Horton, R. "African Conversion"   *Africa* 41 (2), 1971, pp. 85-109.
Horton, R. and Peel, J.D.Y. "Conversion and Confusion: A Rejoinder on Christianity in Eastern Nigeria"   *Canadian Journal of African Studies* 10 (3), 1976, pp. 481-498.
Mbiti, J.S. *African Religions and Philosophy.* London: Heinemann, 1969.
Parsons, T. "Introduction" in Max Weber, *The Sociology of Religion,* Boston: Beacon Press, 1968.
Sundkler, B.G.M. *Bantu Prophets in South Africa.* London: Oxford University Press, 1961.
Turner, H.W. *African Independent Church.* Oxford: Clarendon Press, 1967.
Weber, M. *The Sociology of Religion,* Boston: Beacon Press, 1963. (First published 1922).
Wishlade, R.L. *Sectariansim in Southern Nyasaland.* London: Oxford University Press, 1965.

SUBJECT INDEX